DEAD SPACE™
LIBERATION

For Dead Space Liberation:
   Producers — Cate Latchford
               Chuck Beaver

For Dead Space:
   VP / EP — Steve Papoutsis
   Creative Director — Ben Wanat
   Art Director — Alex Muscat

Special thanks to:
Beth Pielert
Dino Ignacio
Ellana Fortuna
Erika Peterson
Frank Gibeau
John Riccietello
Justin Porter
Laura Miele
Matt Bendett
Monique Miller
Patrick Soderlund
Peter Moore
Steve Pointon

www.deadspace.com

EA   VISCERAL
GAMES

ART BY

CHRISTOPHER SHY

A CIP catalogue record for this title is available from the British Library.

First edition: February 2013

10 9 8 7 6 5 4 3 2 1

Printed in the USA.

What did you think of this book? We love to hear from our readers. Please email us at: readerfeedback@titanemail.com, or write to us at the above address.

To receive advance information, news, competitions, and exclusive offers online, please sign up for the Titan newsletter on our website: www.titanbooks.com

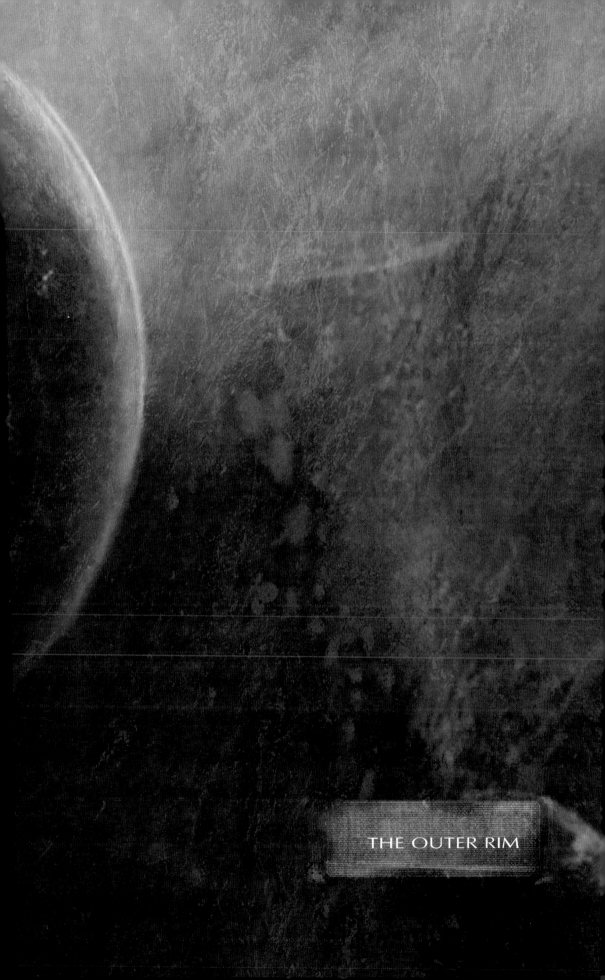

THE OUTER RIM

SUBJECT

PLANET **UXOR**

COMPOSITION: 90 OXIDE 10 IRON

MASS: 5.9736·10^24 KG

MEAN RADIUS: 62710 KM

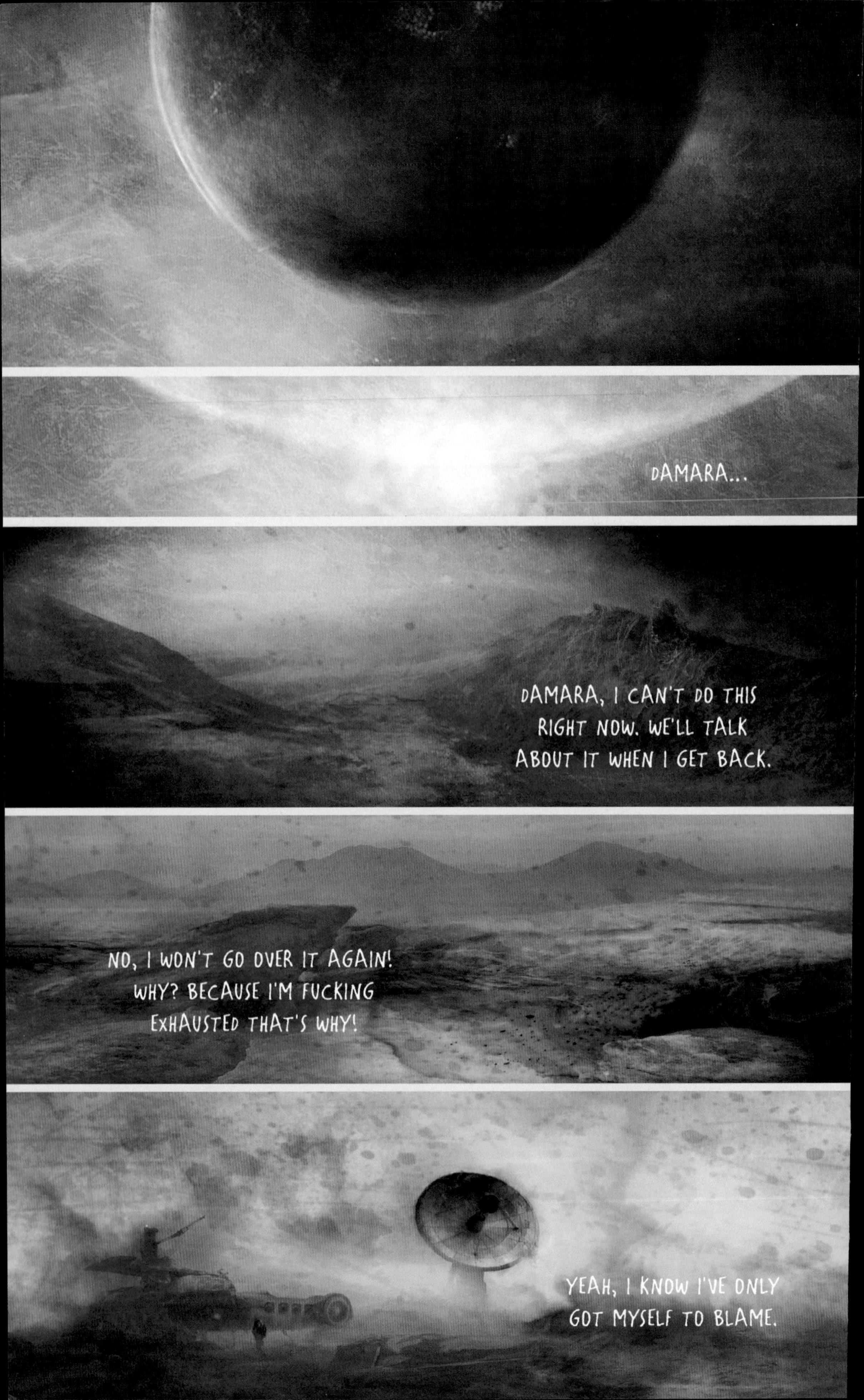
DAMARA...
DAMARA, I CAN'T DO THIS RIGHT NOW. WE'LL TALK ABOUT IT WHEN I GET BACK.
NO, I WON'T GO OVER IT AGAIN! WHY? BECAUSE I'M FUCKING EXHAUSTED THAT'S WHY!
YEAH, I KNOW I'VE ONLY GOT MYSELF TO BLAME.

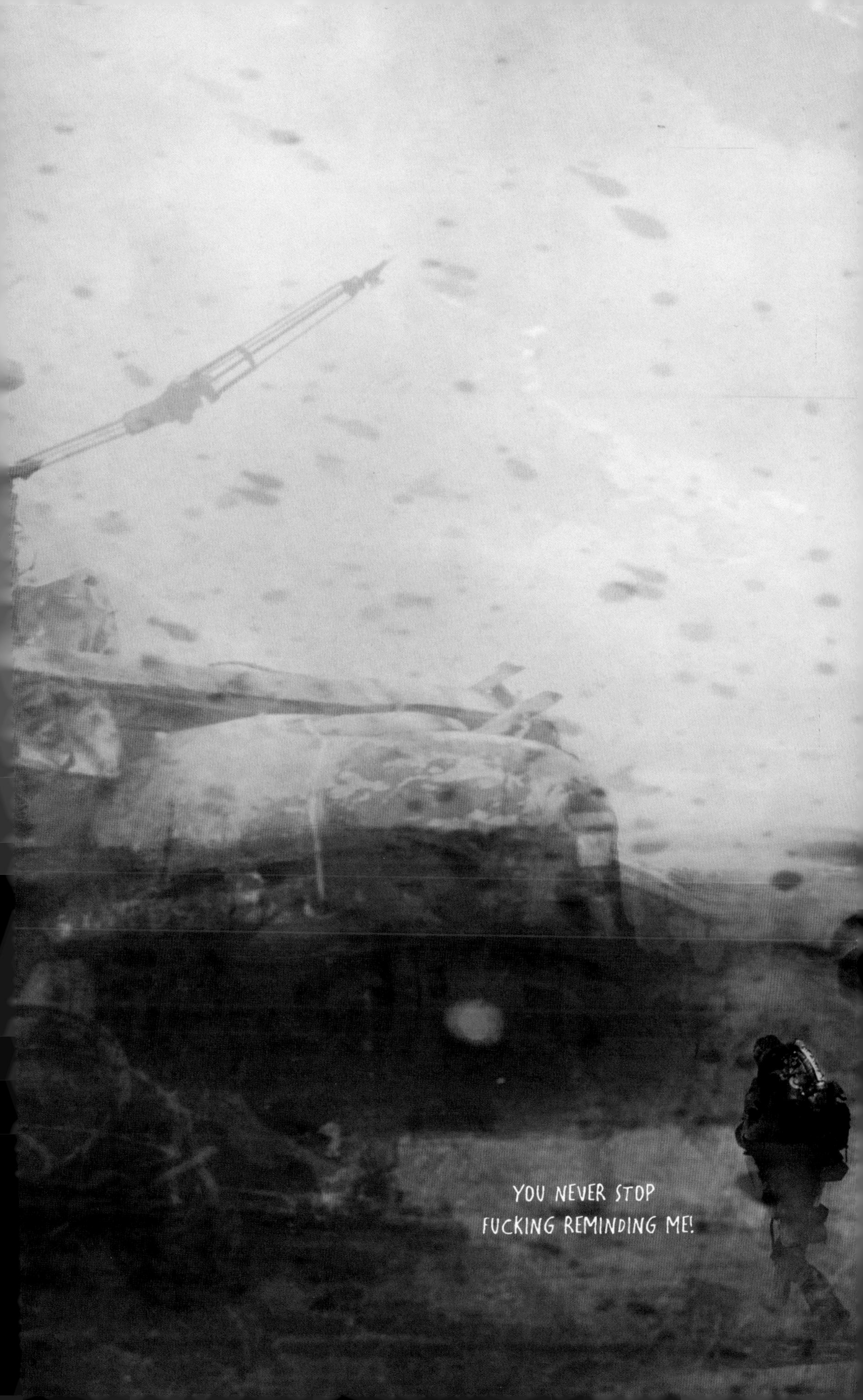
YOU NEVER STOP
FUCKING REMINDING ME!

I'M SORRY. THAT WASN'T FAIR, BUT JUST CUT ME SOME SLACK, OKAY?
I'VE BEEN ON PATROL EIGHTEEN HOURS STRAIGHT.

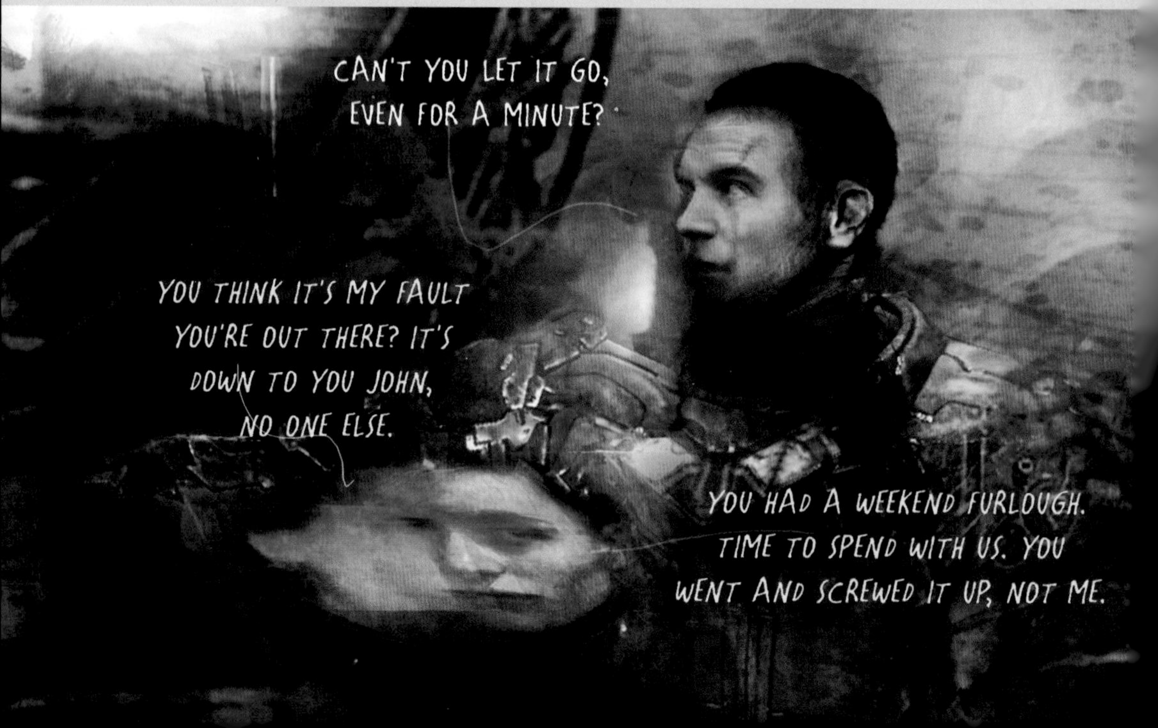
CAN'T YOU LET IT GO, EVEN FOR A MINUTE?
YOU THINK IT'S MY FAULT YOU'RE OUT THERE? IT'S DOWN TO YOU JOHN, NO ONE ELSE.
YOU HAD A WEEKEND FURLOUGH. TIME TO SPEND WITH US. YOU WENT AND SCREWED IT UP, NOT ME.

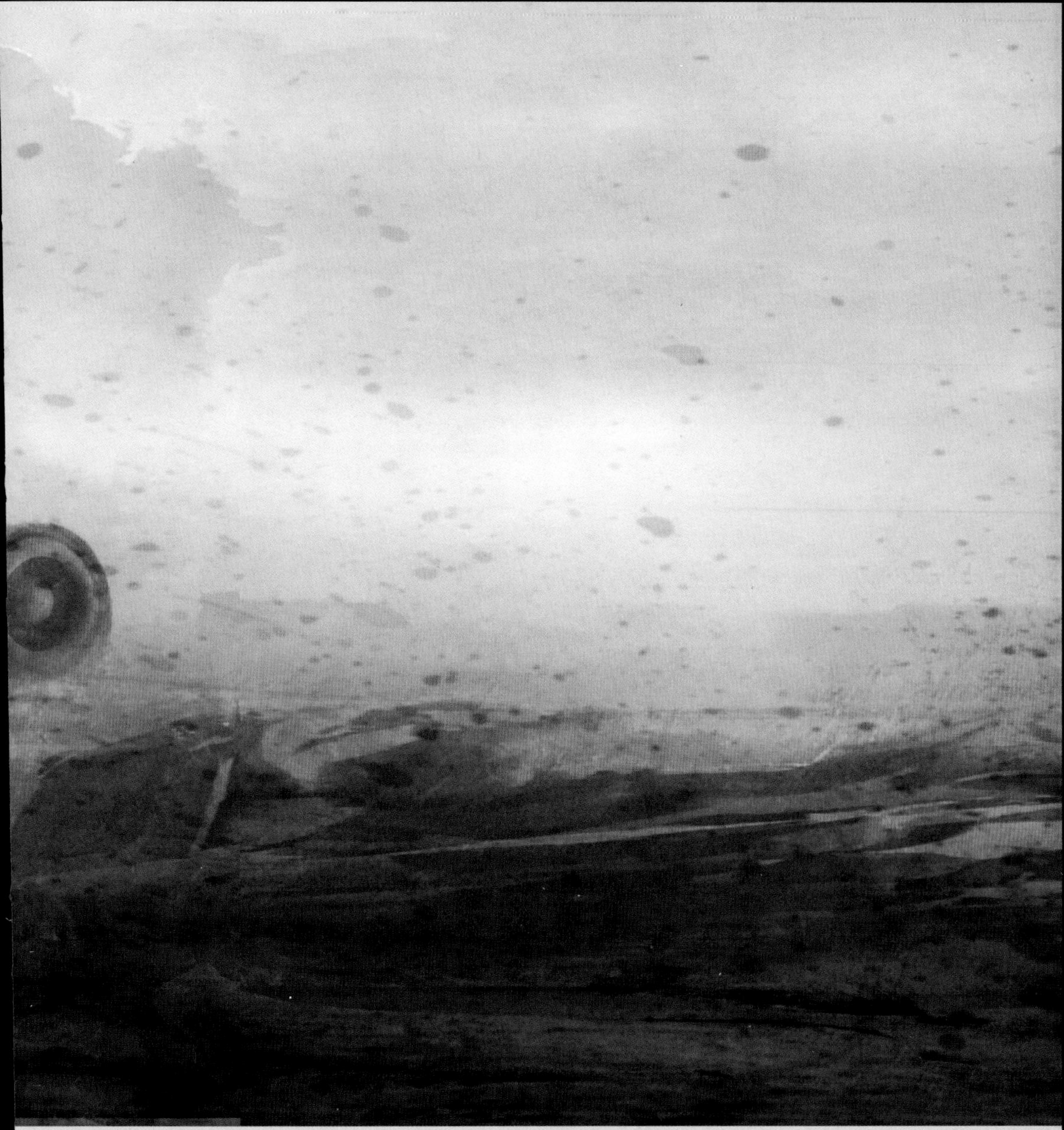

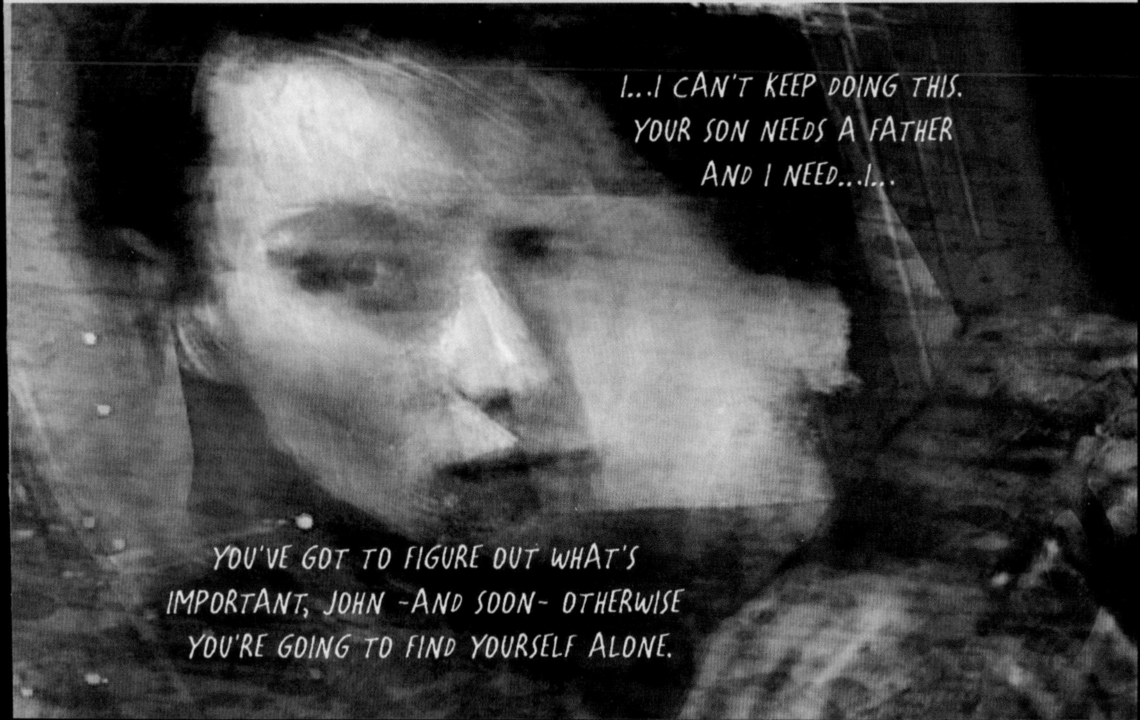
I...I CAN'T KEEP DOING THIS. YOUR SON NEEDS A FATHER AND I NEED...I...
YOU'VE GOT TO FIGURE OUT WHAT'S IMPORTANT, JOHN -AND SOON- OTHERWISE YOU'RE GOING TO FIND YOURSELF ALONE.

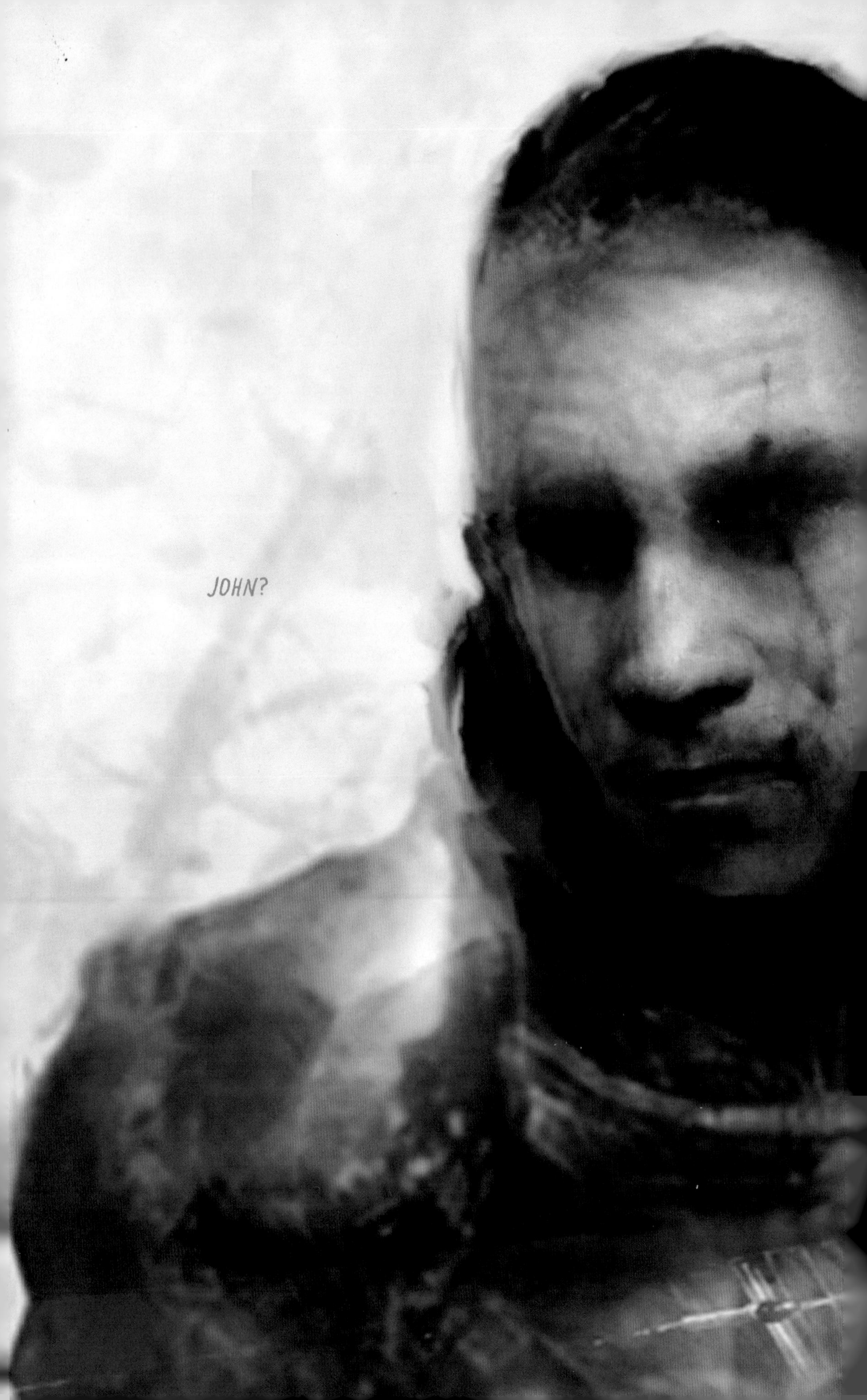
JOHN?

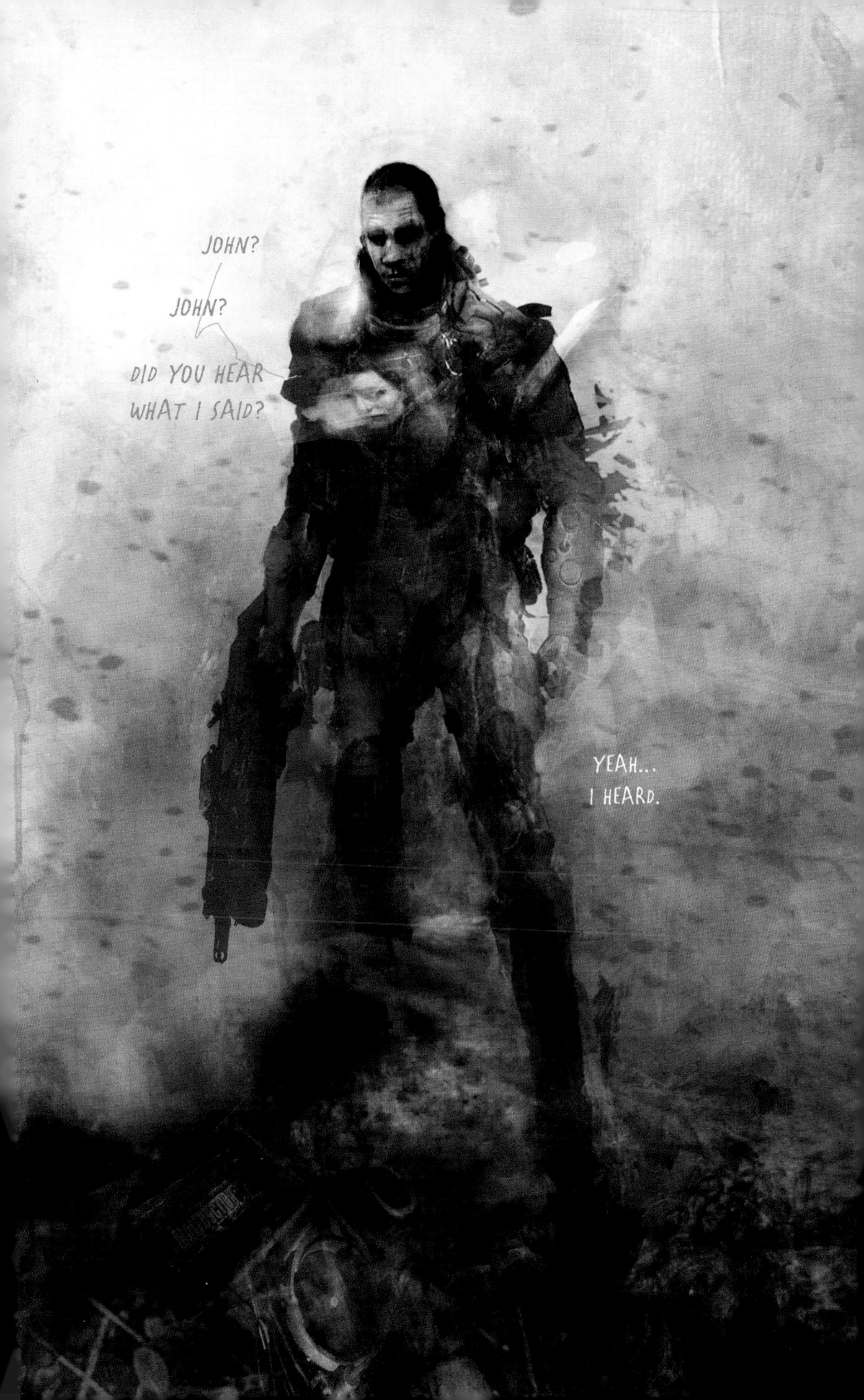
JOHN?
JOHN?
DID YOU HEAR WHAT I SAID?
YEAH... I HEARD.

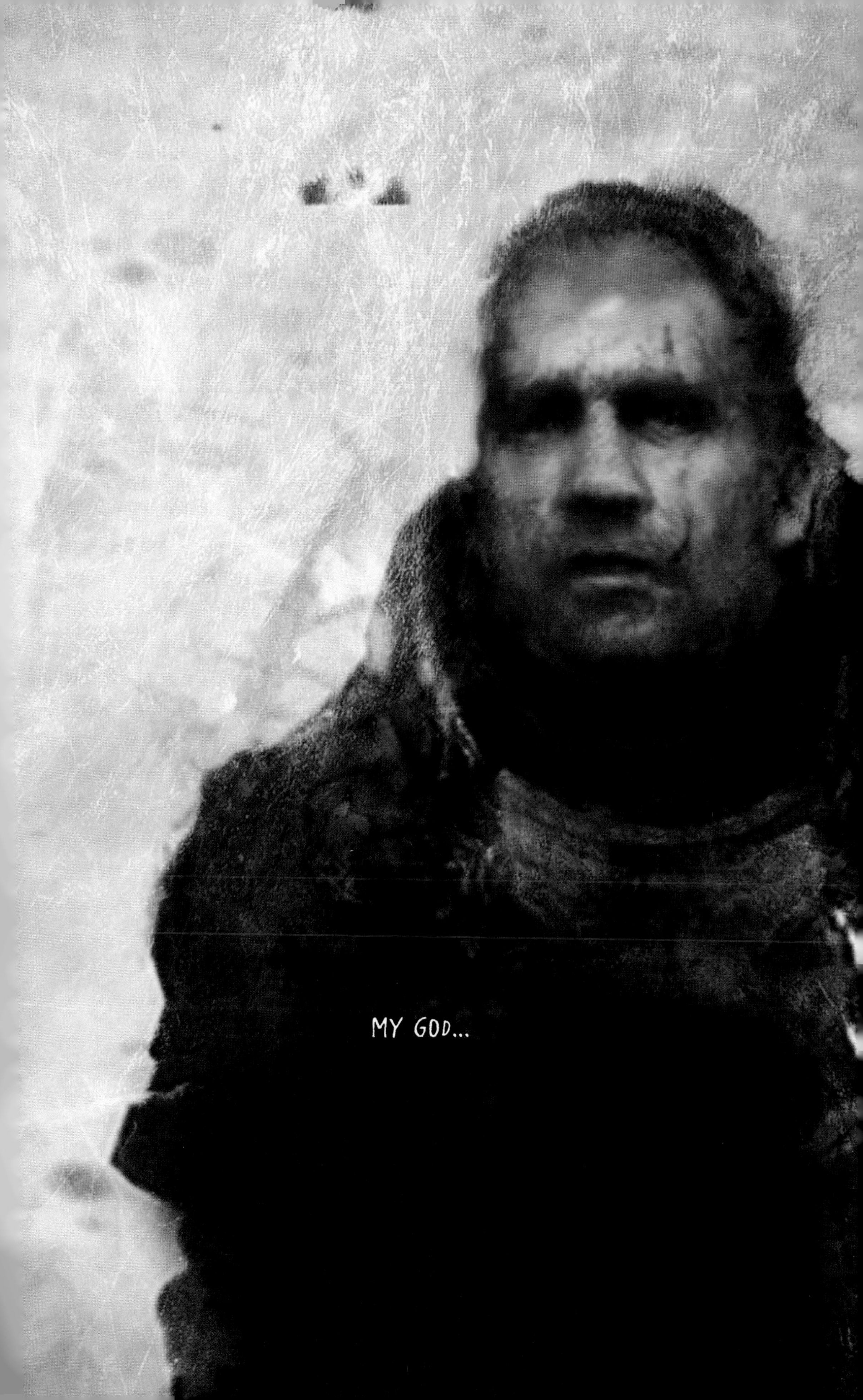
MY GOD...

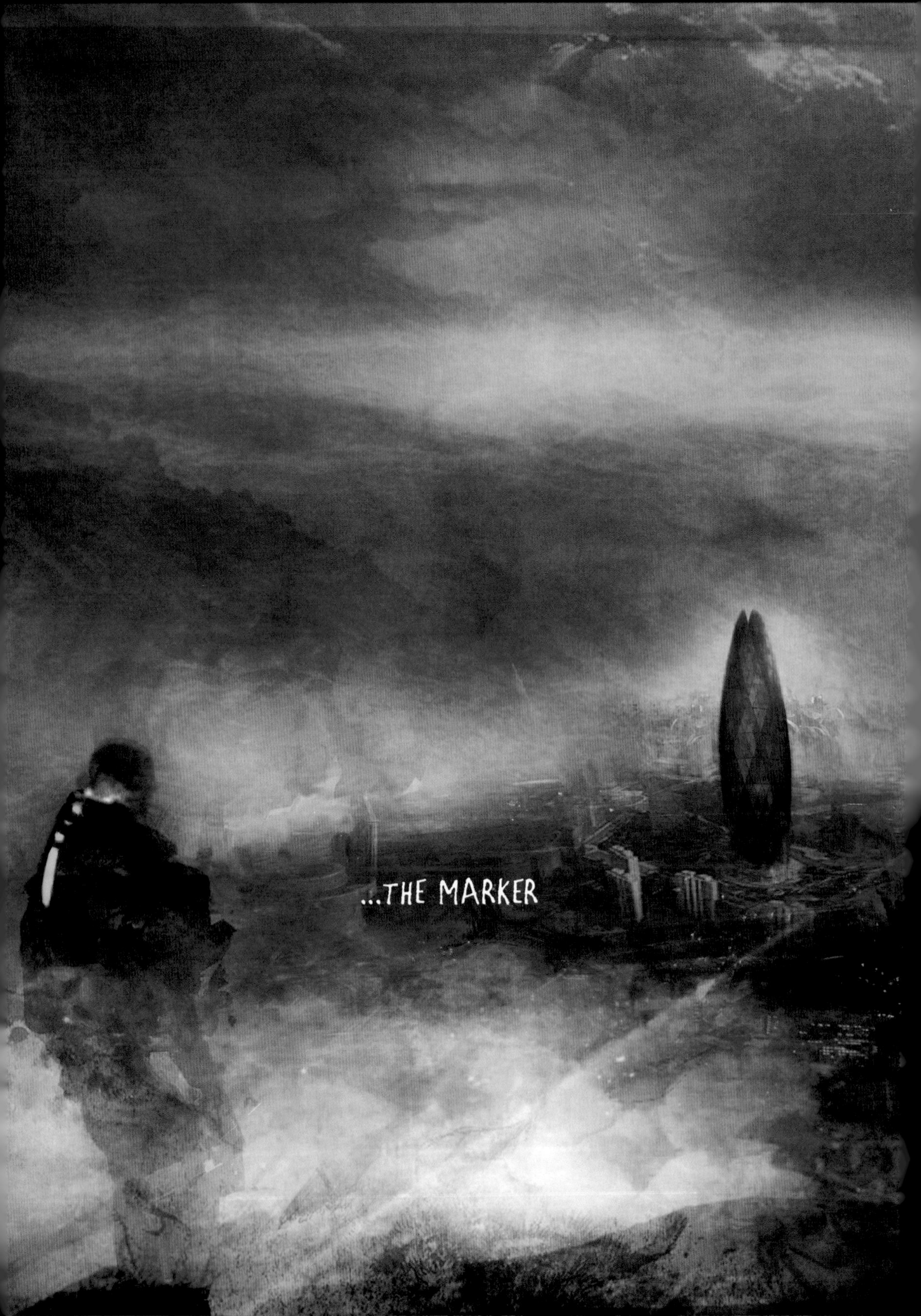
...THE MARKER

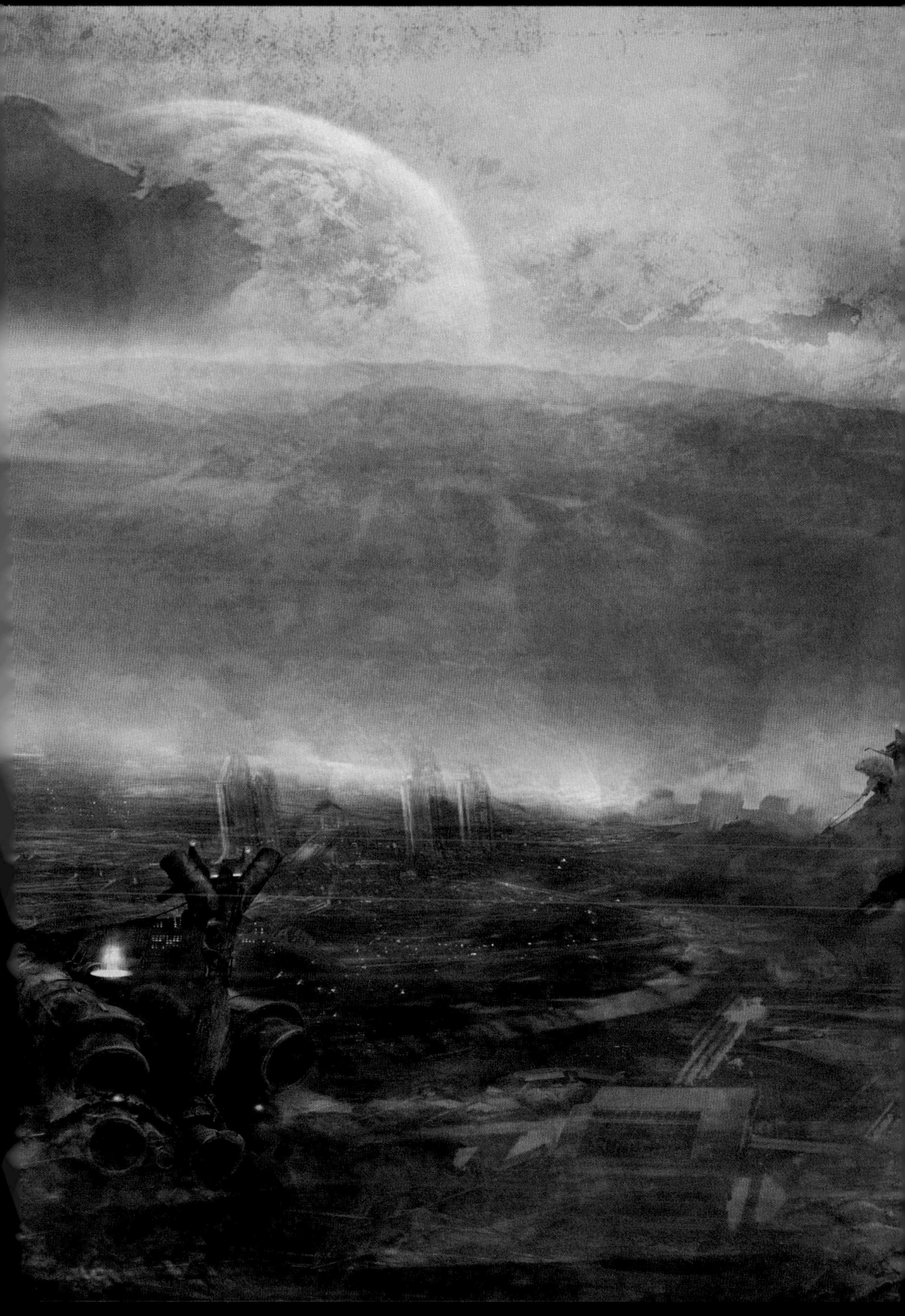

DAMARA!
YOU THINK YOU CAN JUST -
SHUT UP AND LISTEN! GRAB DYLAN AND GO DOWN TO THE BLAST SHELTER!
JOHN, WHAT'RE YOU -
GO, NOW! BEFORE IT'S --
-- TOO LATE!
DAMARA!

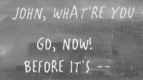

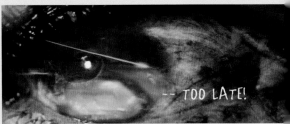

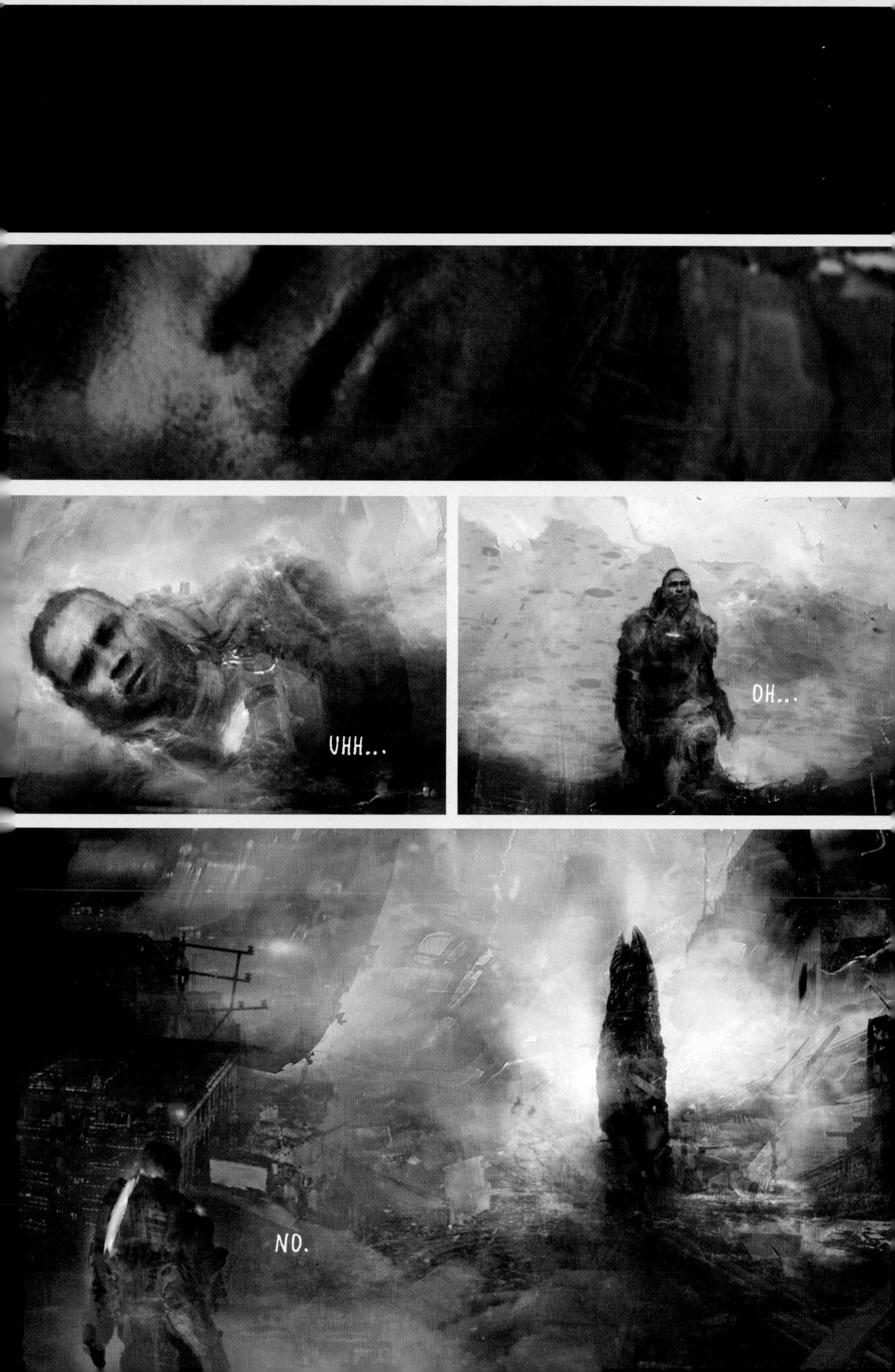
UHH...
OH...
NO.

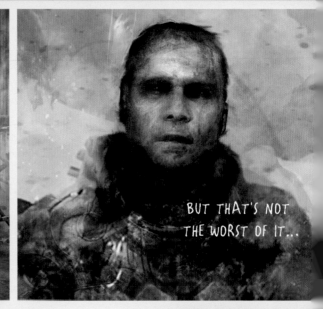

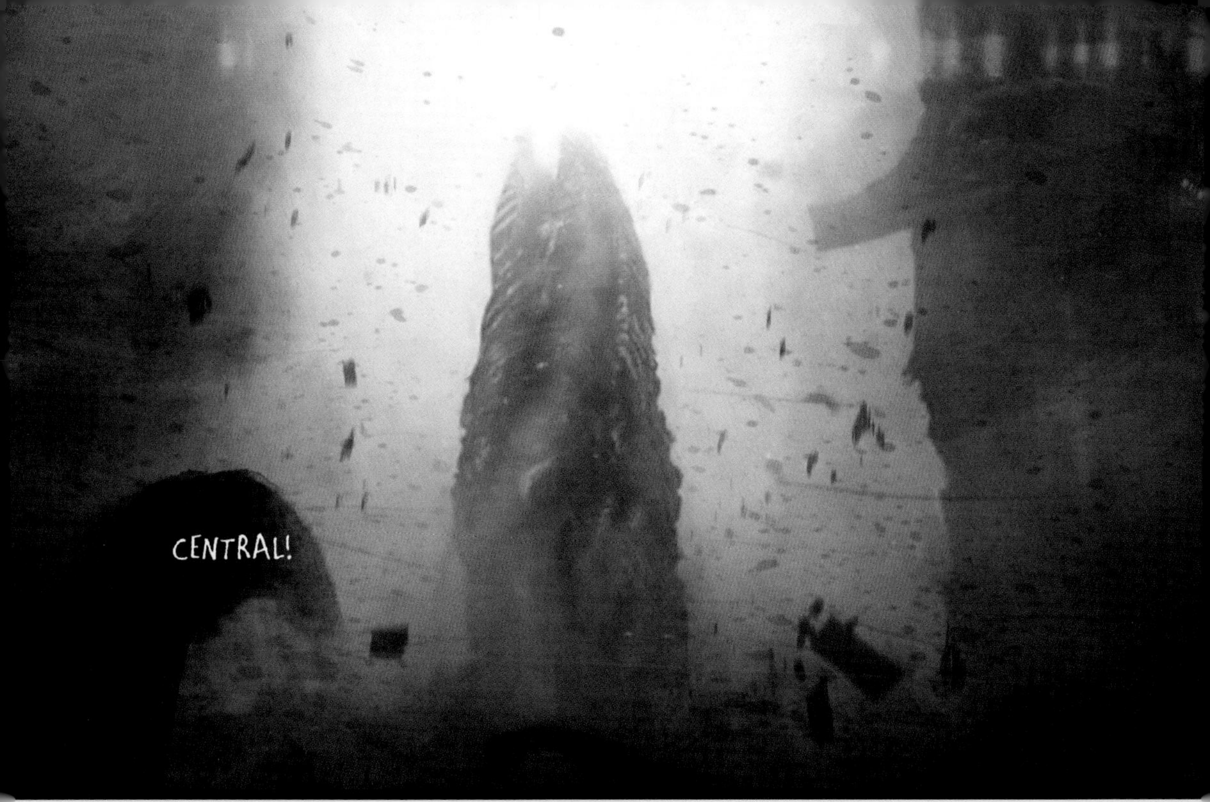
CENTRAL!
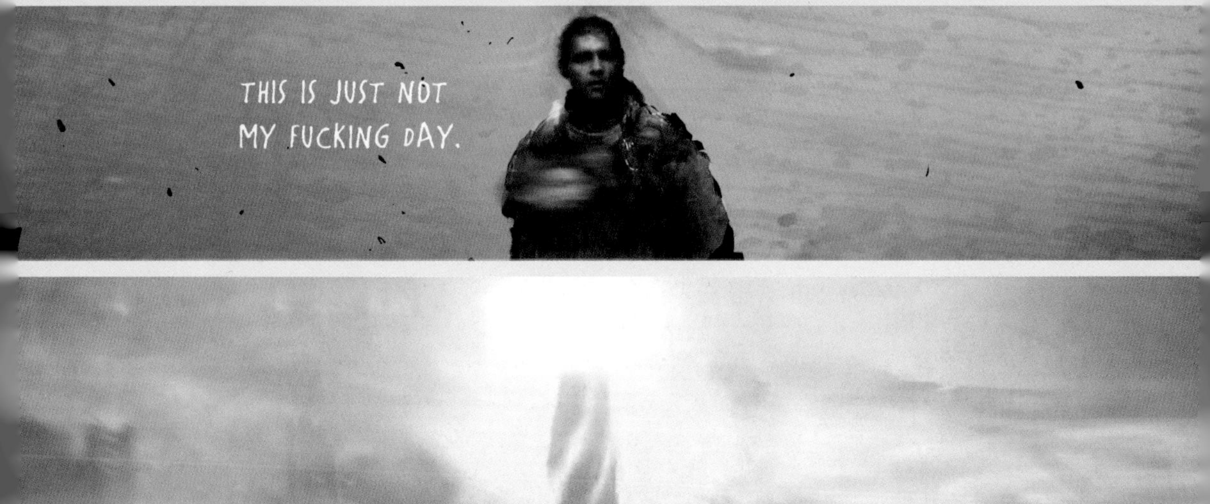
THIS IS JUST NOT
MY FUCKING DAY.
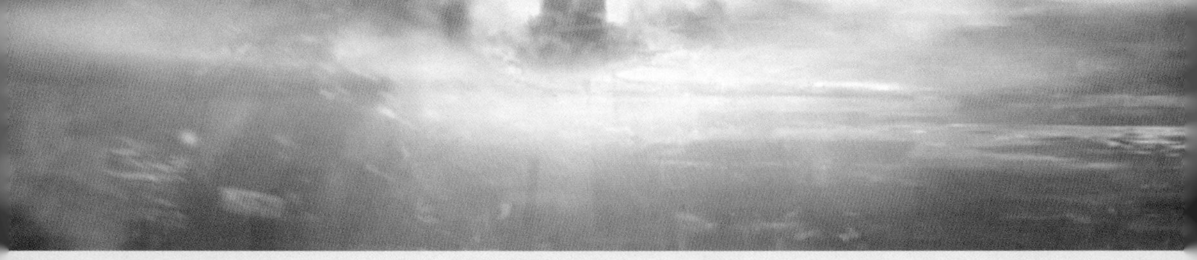
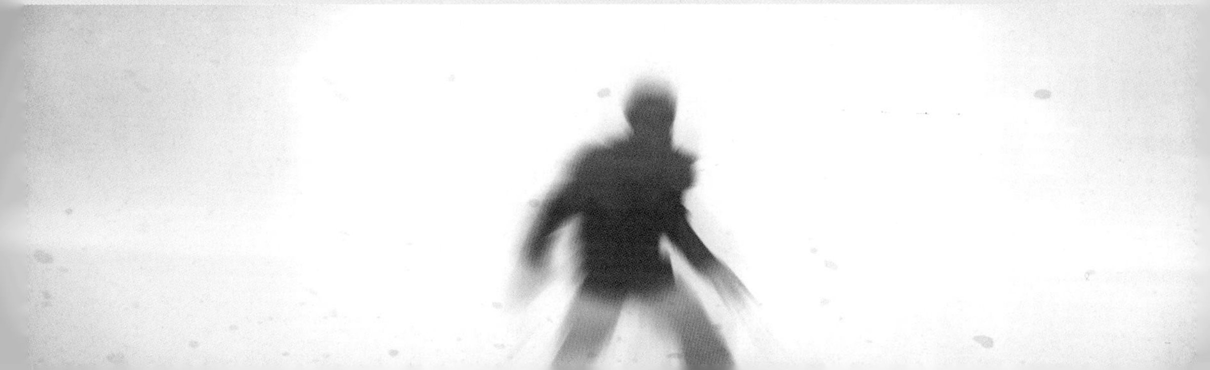

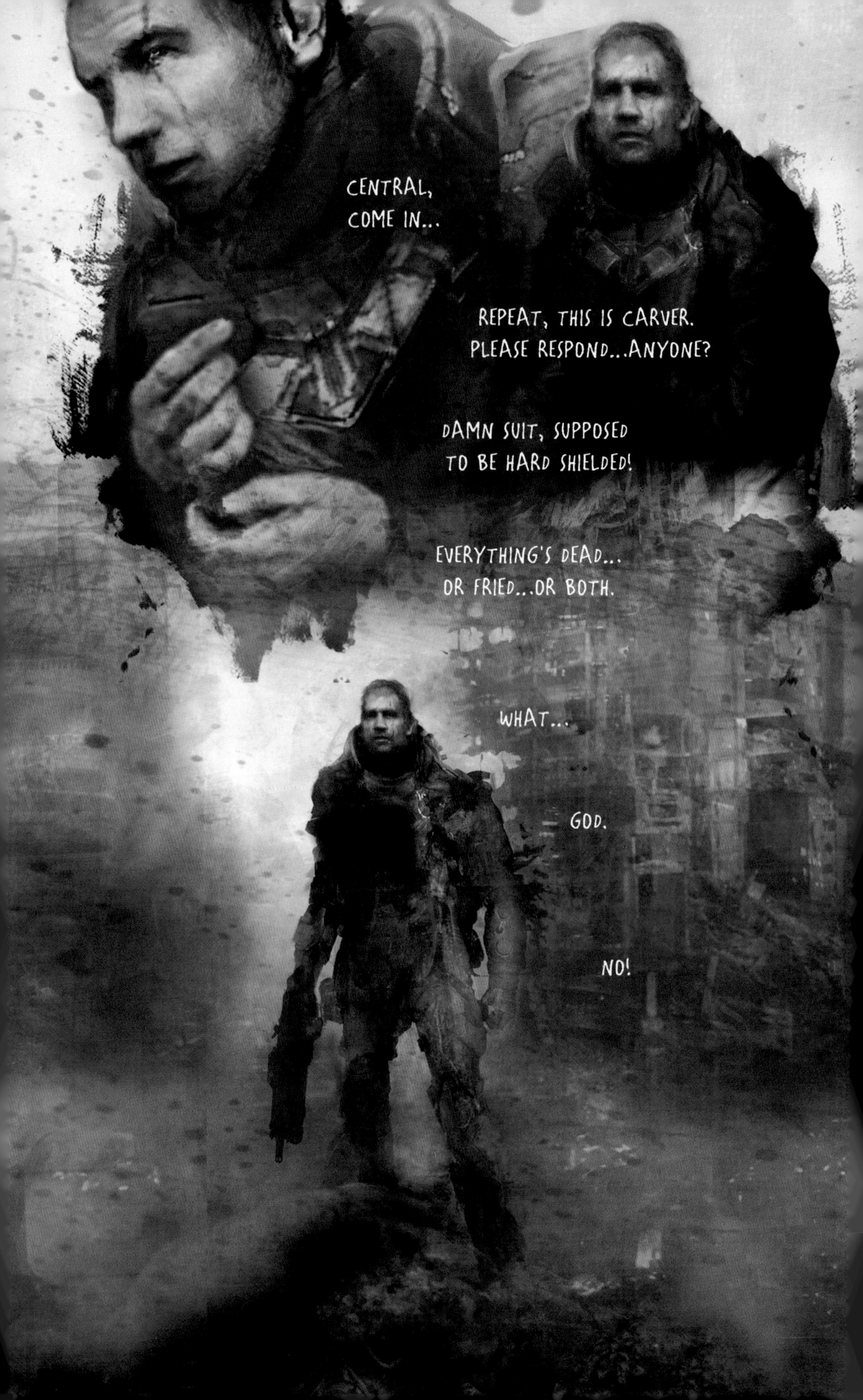
CENTRAL, COME IN...
REPEAT, THIS IS CARVER. PLEASE RESPOND...ANYONE?
DAMN SUIT, SUPPOSED TO BE HARD SHIELDED!
EVERYTHING'S DEAD... OR FRIED...OR BOTH.
WHAT...
GOD.
NO!

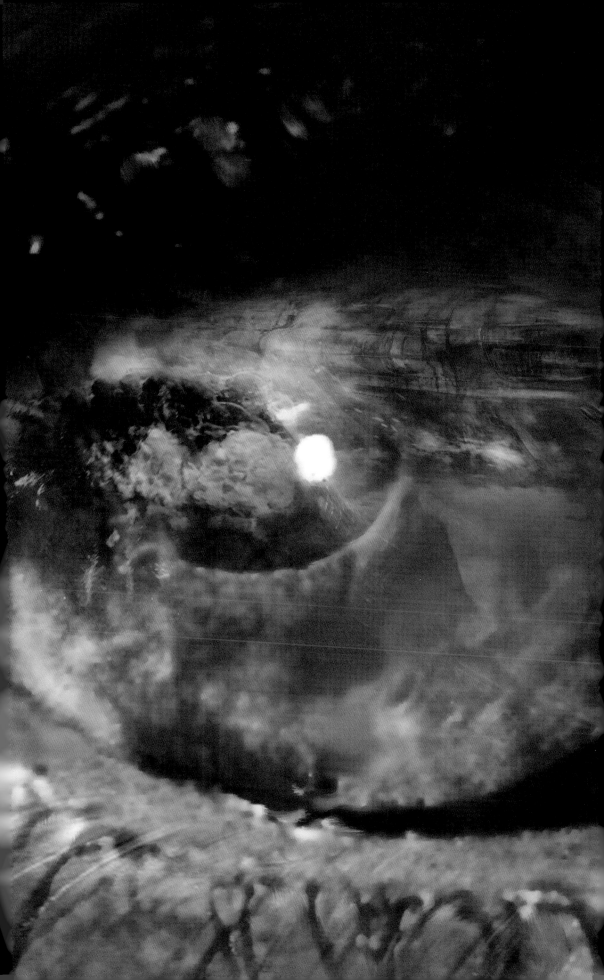

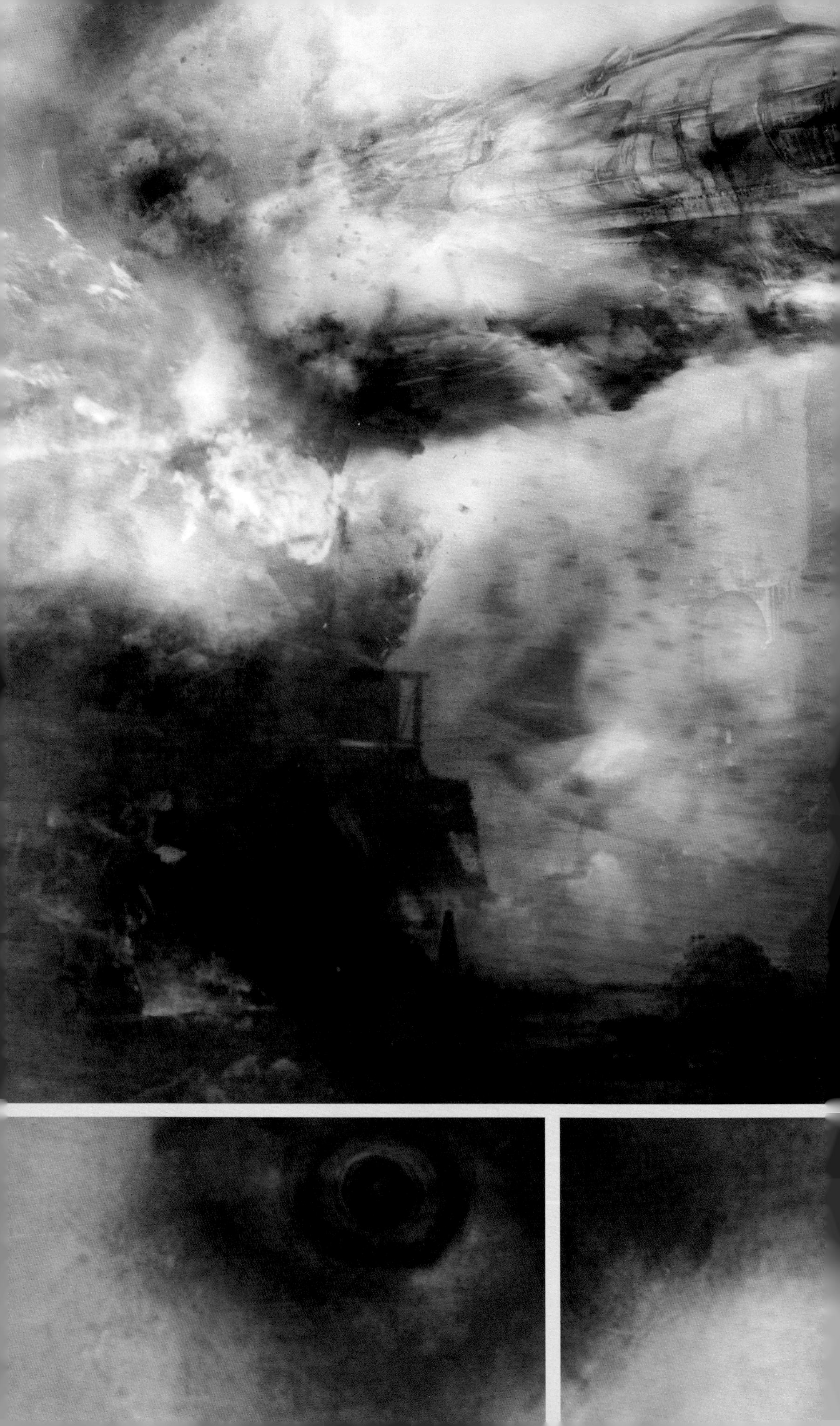

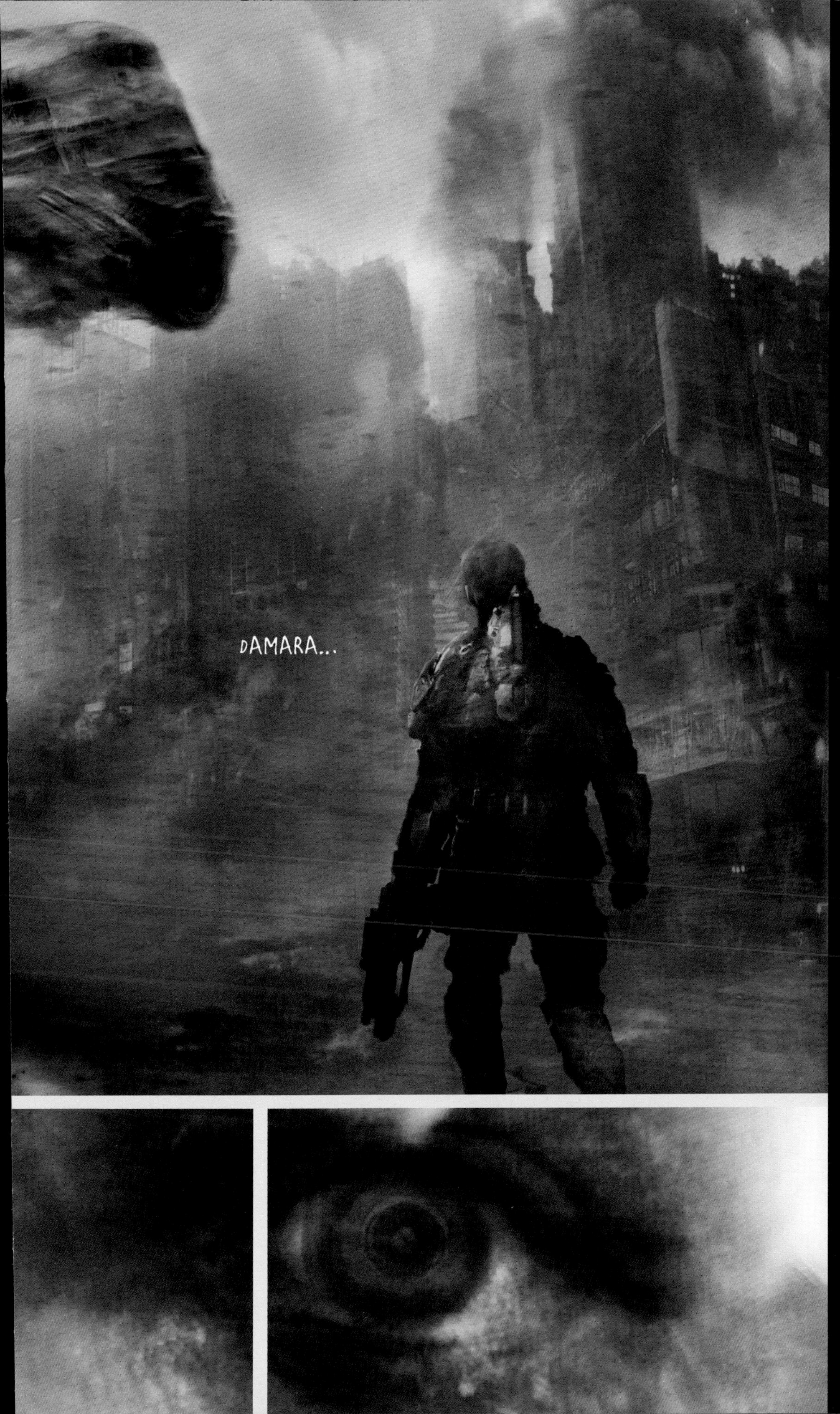
DAMARA...

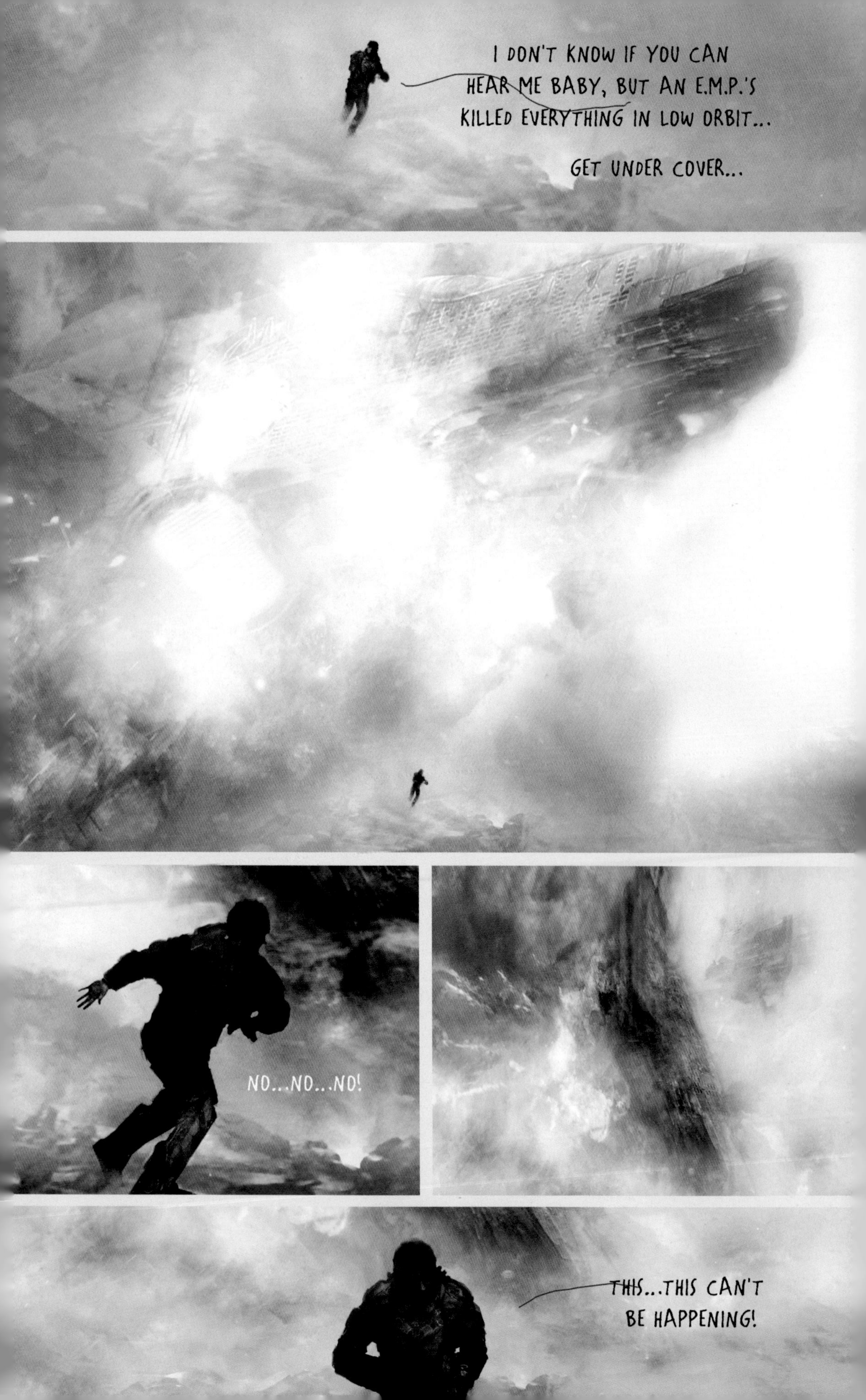
I DON'T KNOW IF YOU CAN HEAR ME BABY, BUT AN E.M.P.'S KILLED EVERYTHING IN LOW ORBIT...
GET UNDER COVER...
NO...NO...NO!
THIS...THIS CAN'T BE HAPPENING!

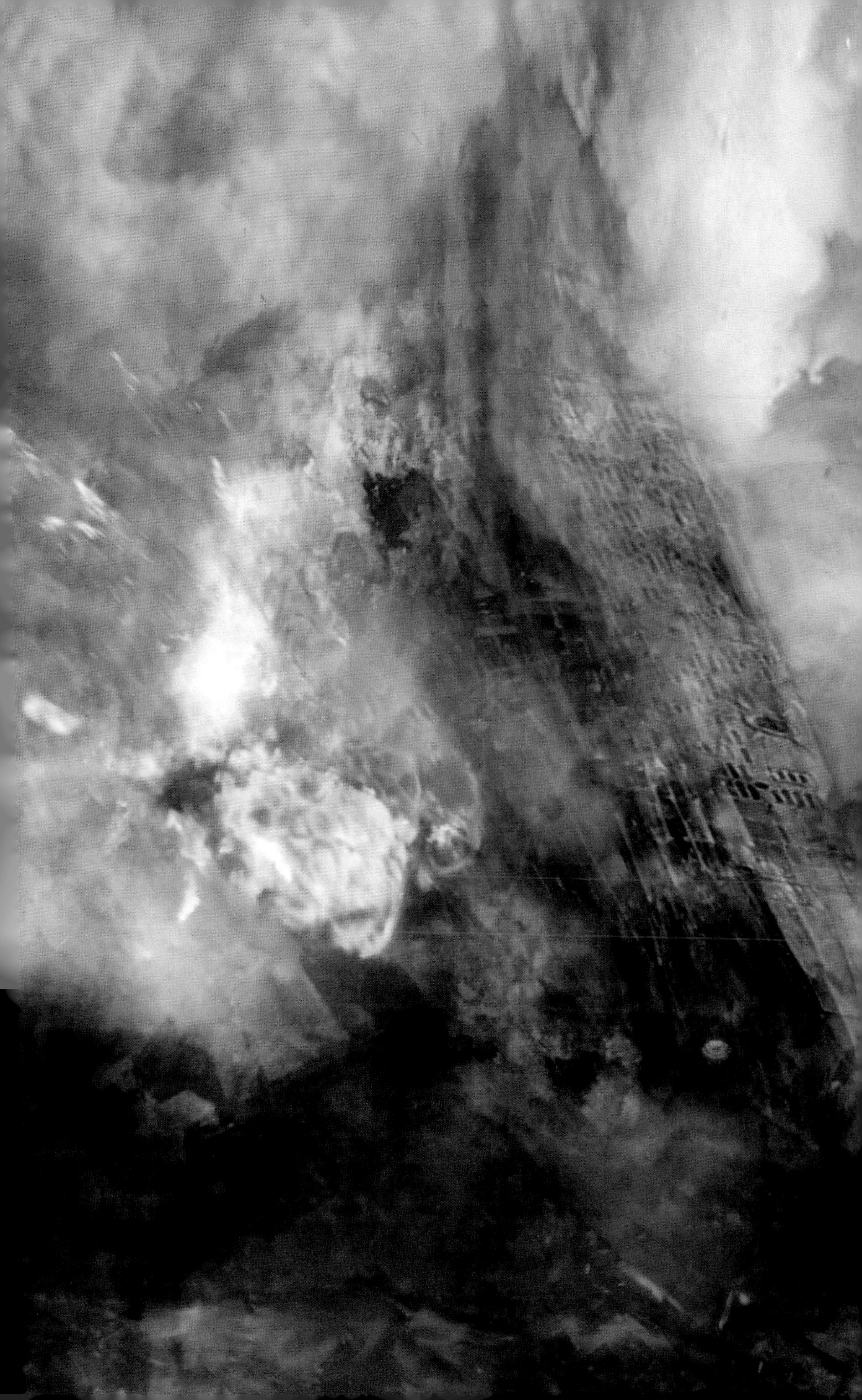

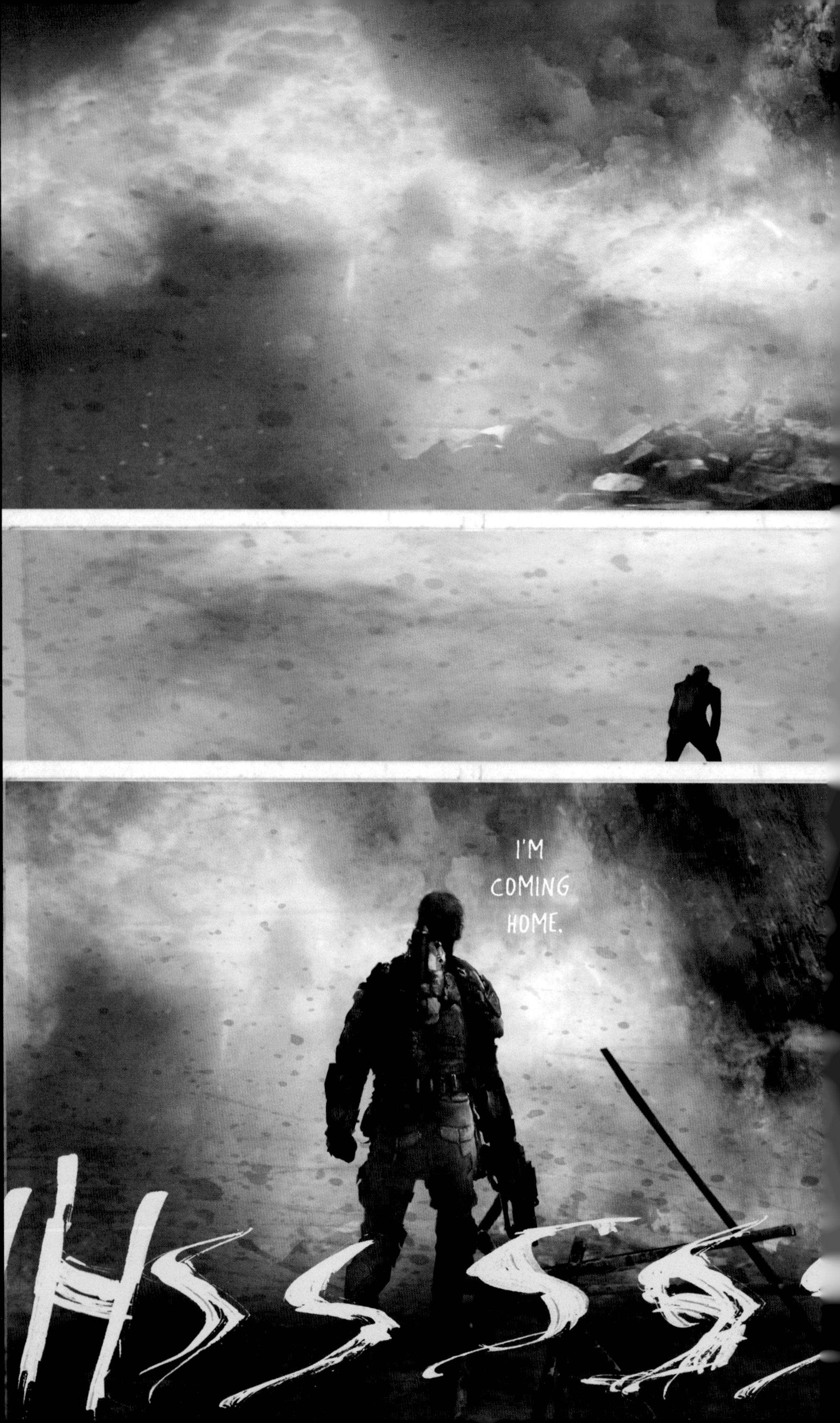
I'M COMING HOME.

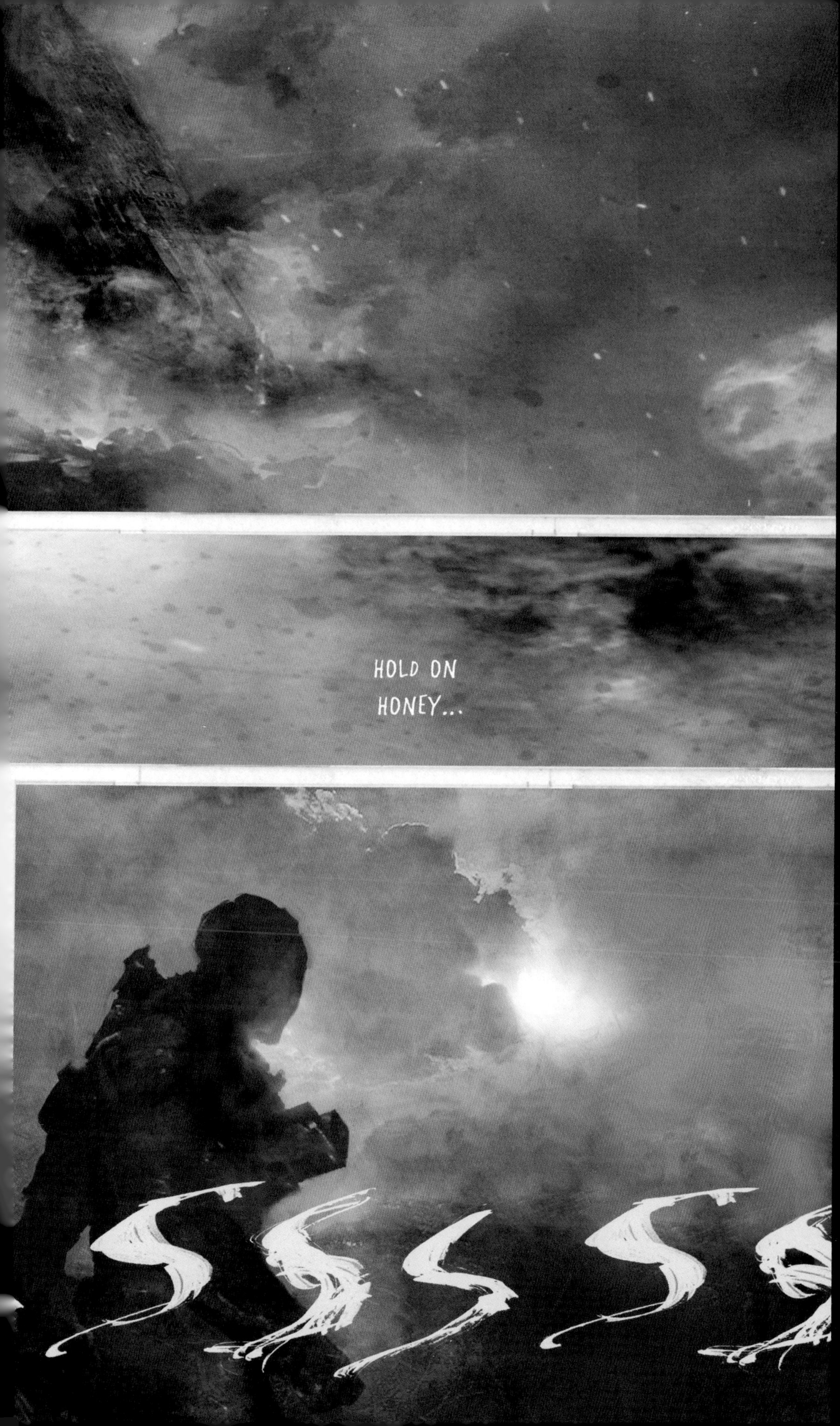
HOLD ON
HONEY...
SSSSS

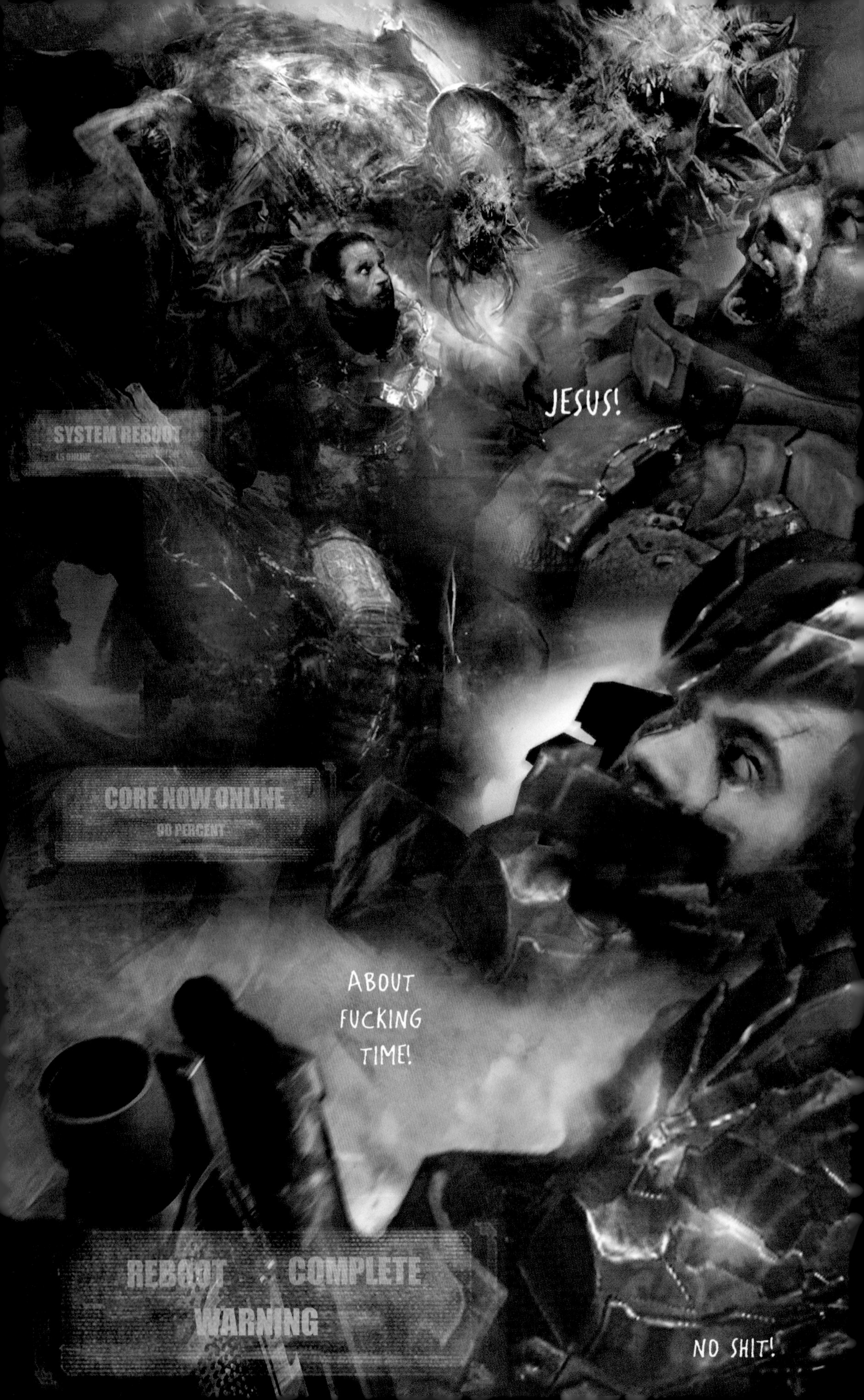
SYSTEM REBOOT
JESUS!
CORE NOW ONLINE
90 PERCENT
ABOUT FUCKING TIME!
REBOOT : COMPLETE
WARNING
NO SHIT!

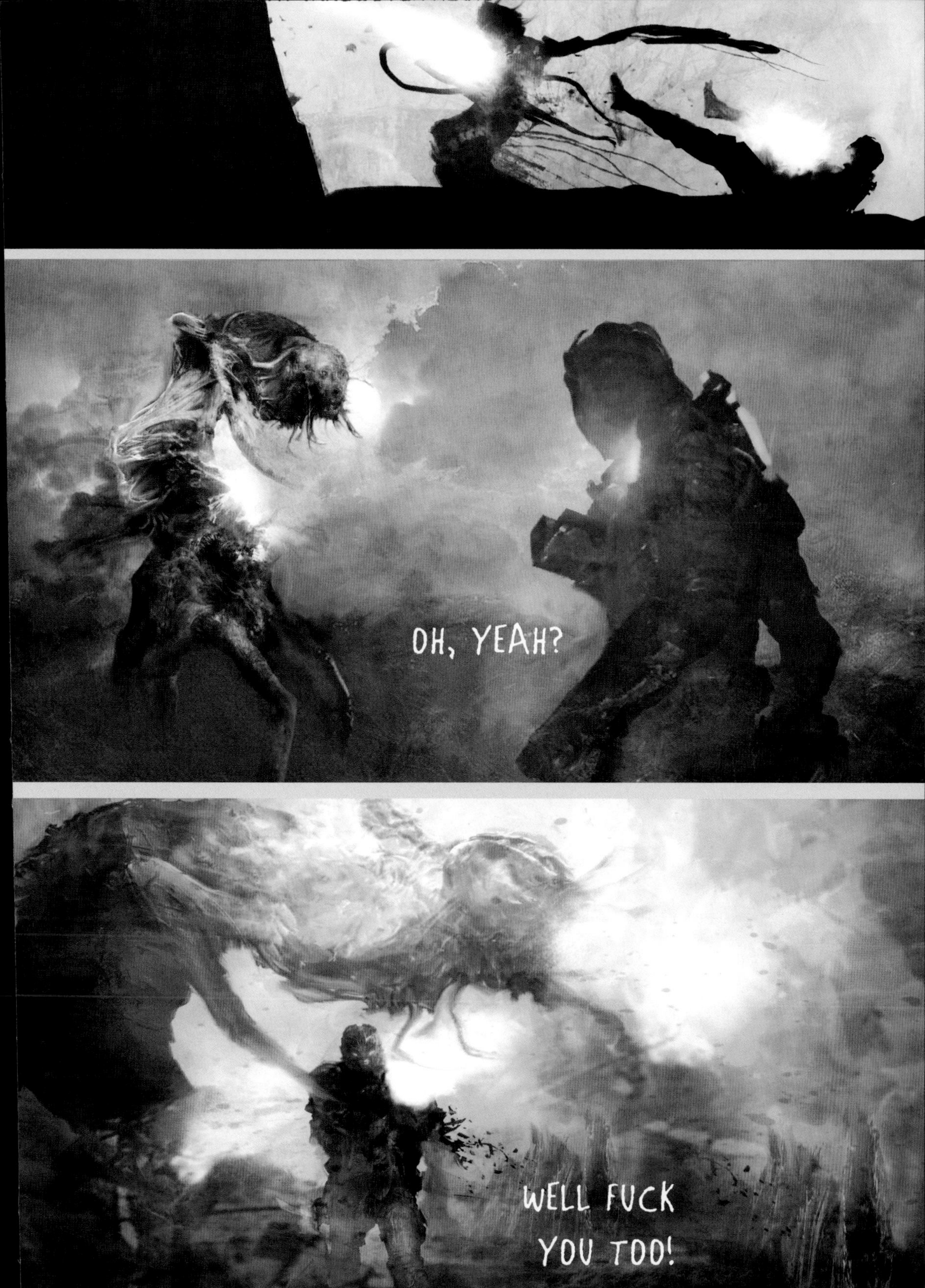
OH, YEAH?
WELL FUCK YOU TOO!

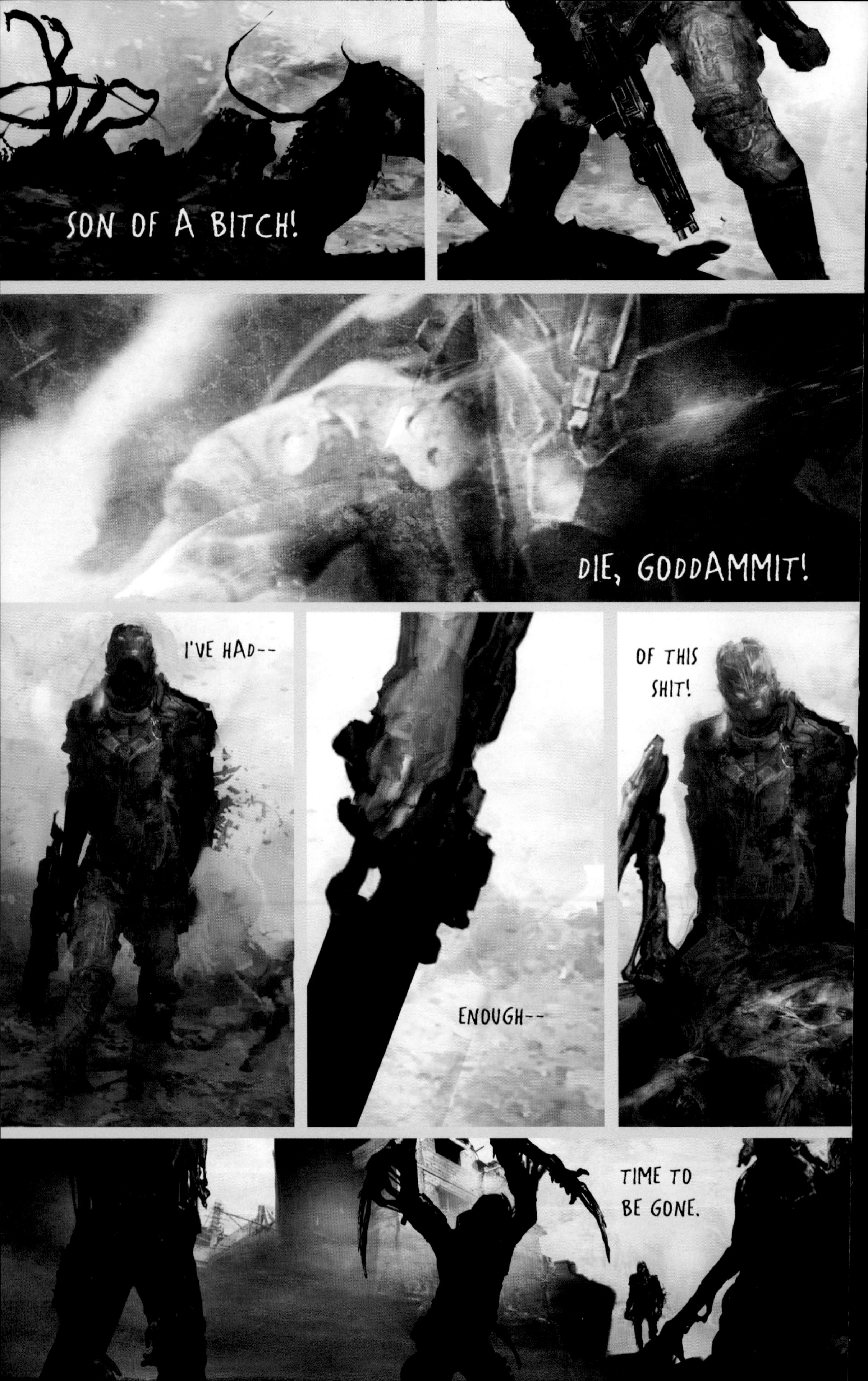
SON OF A BITCH!
DIE, GODDAMMIT!
I'VE HAD--
ENOUGH--
OF THIS SHIT!
TIME TO BE GONE.

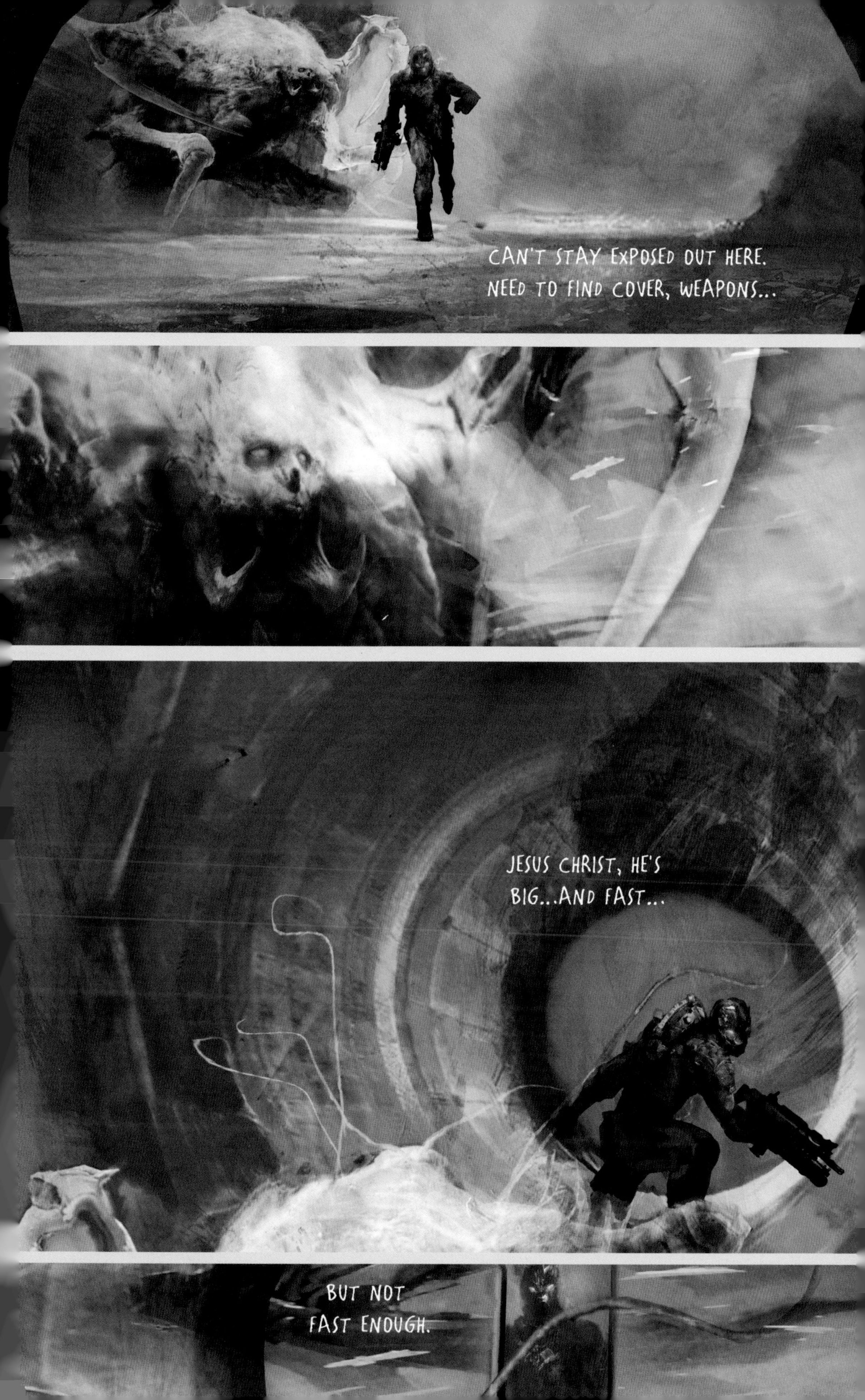
CAN'T STAY EXPOSED OUT HERE.
NEED TO FIND COVER, WEAPONS...
JESUS CHRIST, HE'S
BIG...AND FAST...
BUT NOT
FAST ENOUGH.

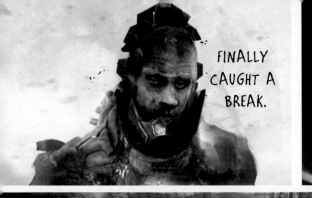

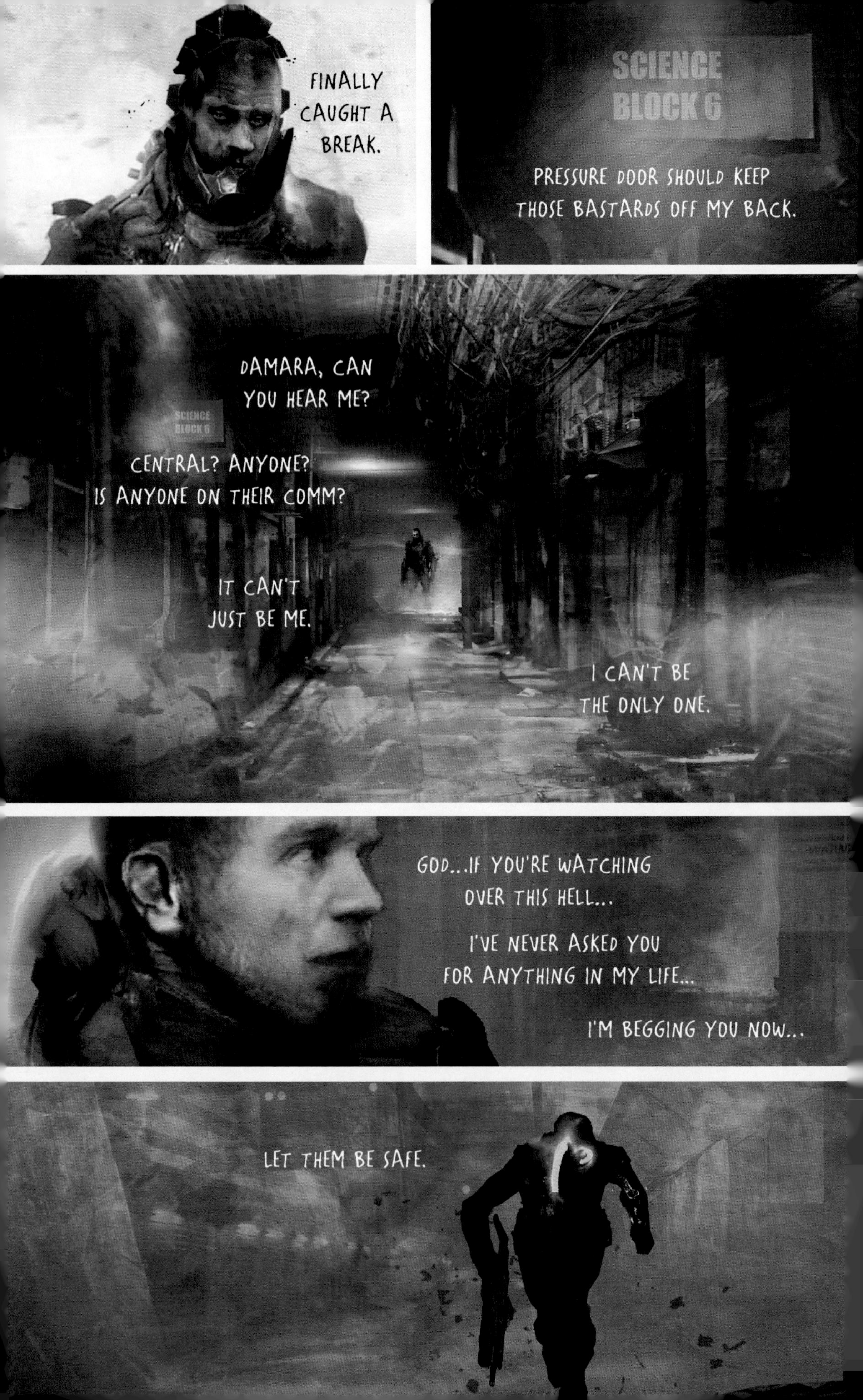
FINALLY CAUGHT A BREAK.
SCIENCE BLOCK 6
PRESSURE DOOR SHOULD KEEP THOSE BASTARDS OFF MY BACK.
DAMARA, CAN YOU HEAR ME?
SCIENCE BLOCK 6
CENTRAL? ANYONE? IS ANYONE ON THEIR COMM?
IT CAN'T JUST BE ME.
I CAN'T BE THE ONLY ONE.
GOD...IF YOU'RE WATCHING OVER THIS HELL...
I'VE NEVER ASKED YOU FOR ANYTHING IN MY LIFE...
I'M BEGGING YOU NOW...
LET THEM BE SAFE.

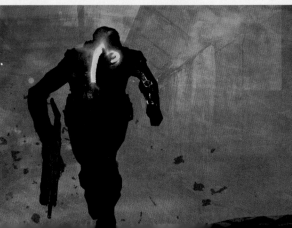

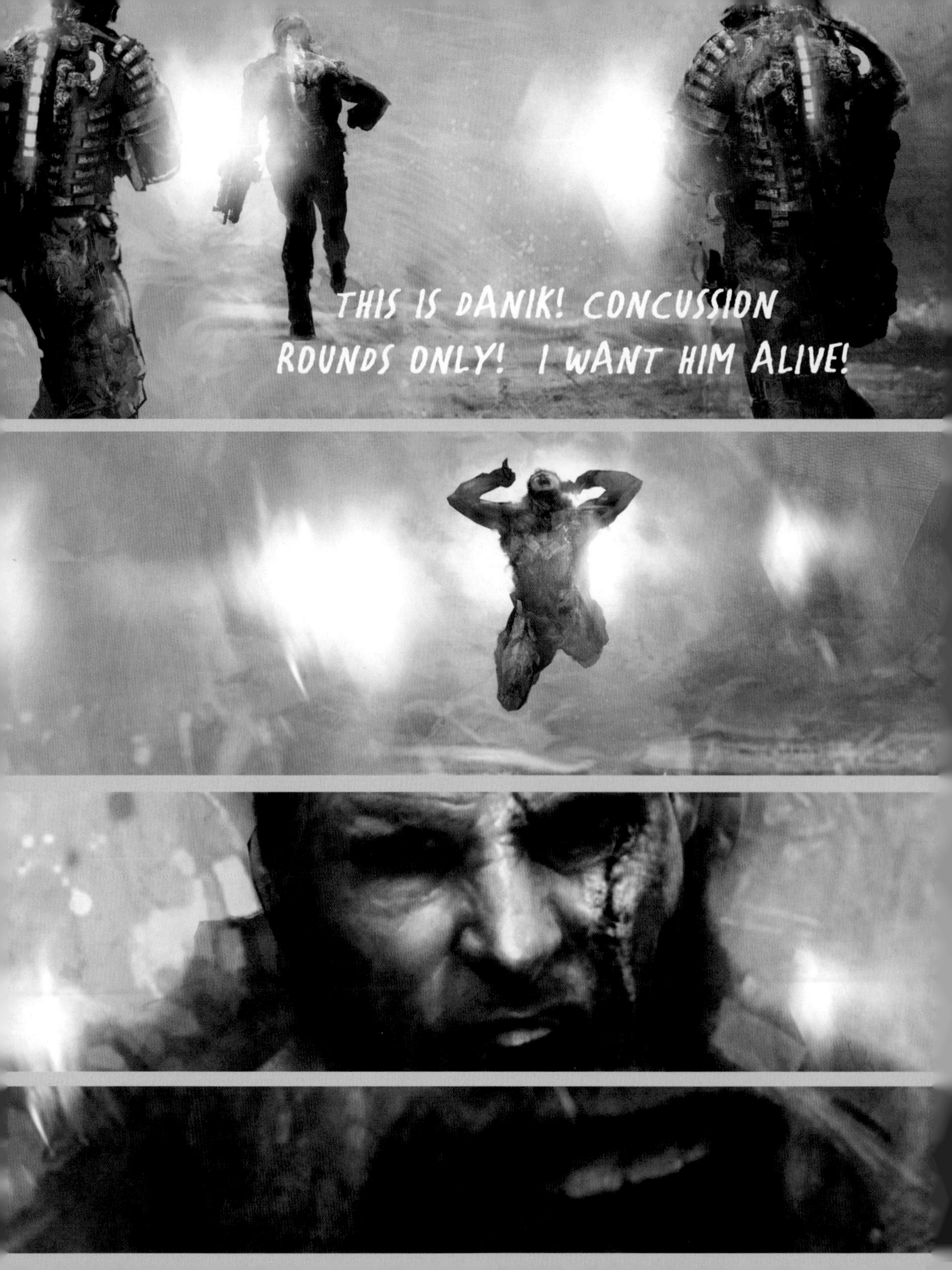
THIS IS DANIK! CONCUSSION ROUNDS ONLY! I WANT HIM ALIVE!

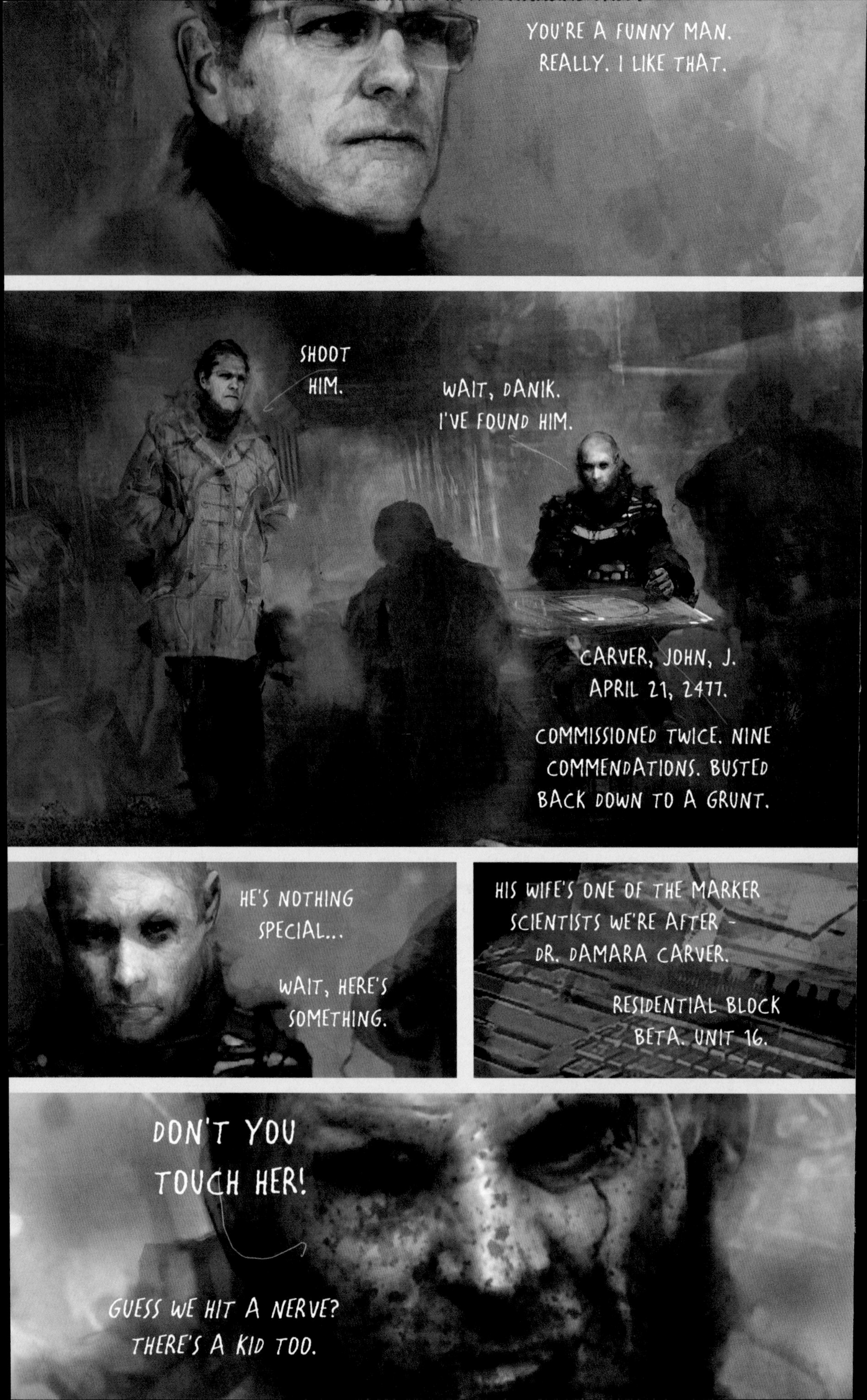
YOU'RE A FUNNY MAN. REALLY. I LIKE THAT.
SHOOT HIM.
WAIT, DANIK. I'VE FOUND HIM.
CARVER, JOHN, J. APRIL 21, 2477.
COMMISSIONED TWICE. NINE COMMENDATIONS. BUSTED BACK DOWN TO A GRUNT.
HE'S NOTHING SPECIAL...
WAIT, HERE'S SOMETHING.
HIS WIFE'S ONE OF THE MARKER SCIENTISTS WE'RE AFTER - DR. DAMARA CARVER.
RESIDENTIAL BLOCK BETA. UNIT 16.
DON'T YOU TOUCH HER!
GUESS WE HIT A NERVE? THERE'S A KID TOO.

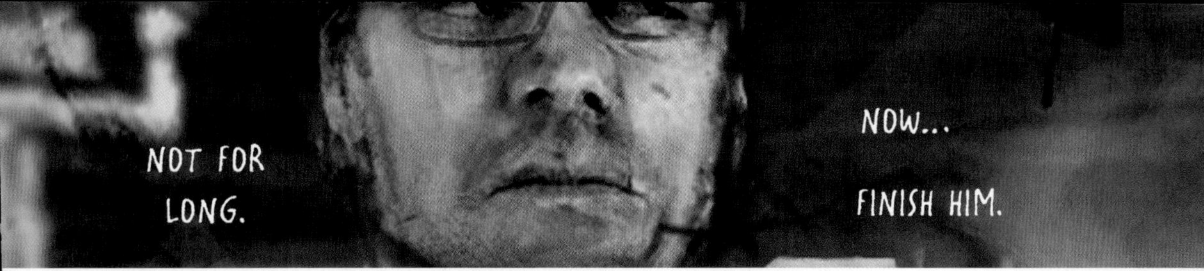
NOT FOR LONG.
NOW...
FINISH HIM.

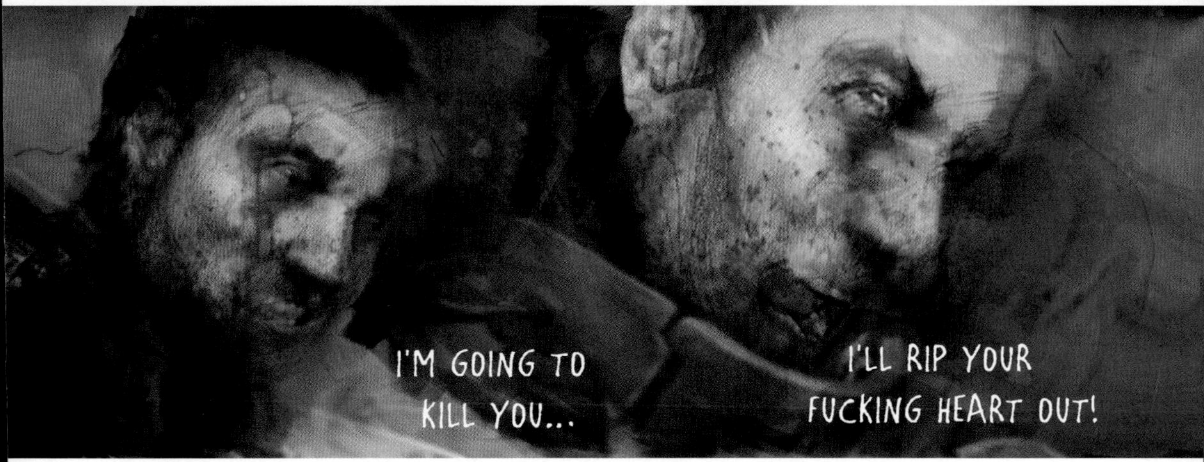
I'M GOING TO KILL YOU...
I'LL RIP YOUR FUCKING HEART OUT!

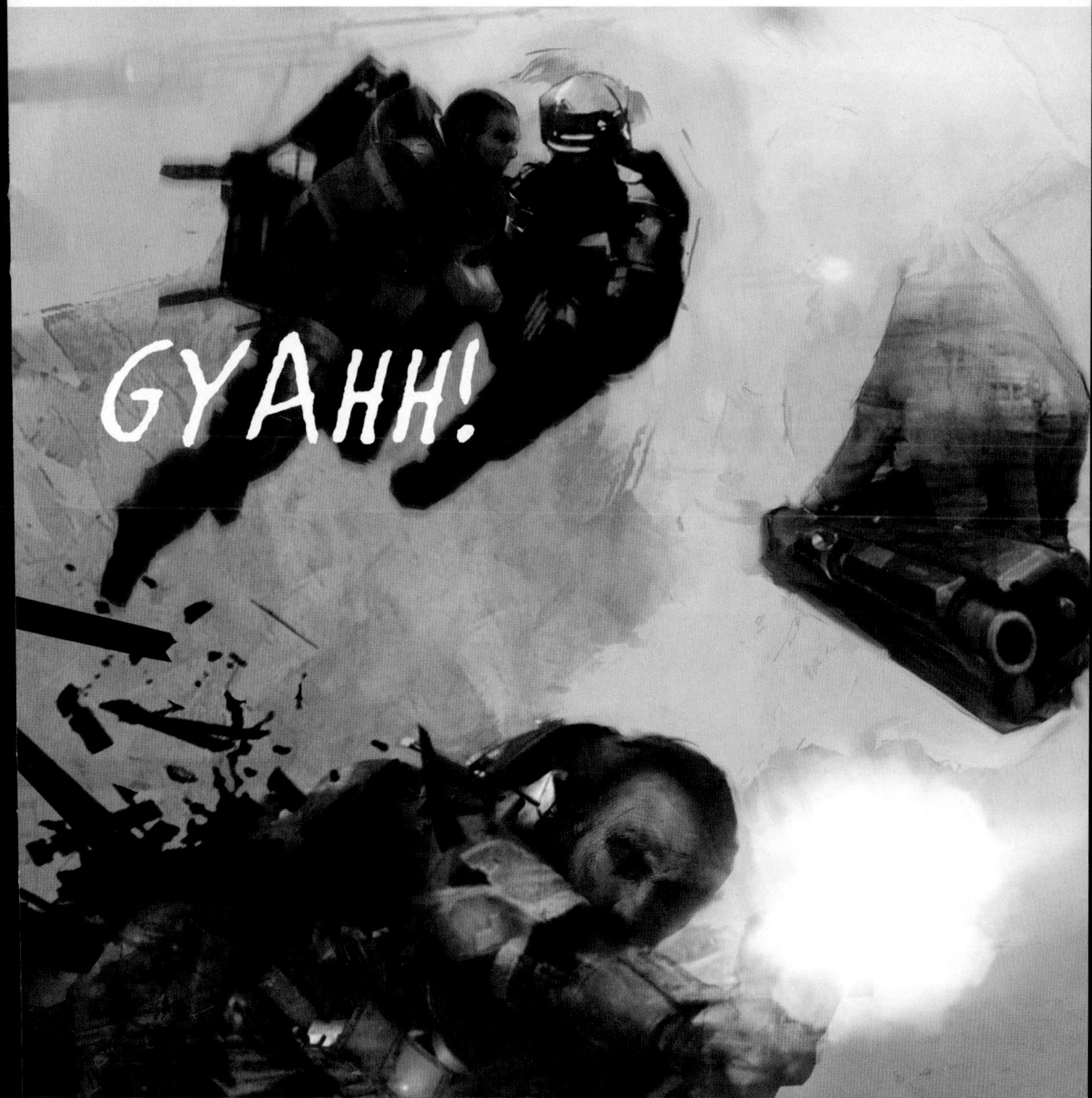
GYAHH!

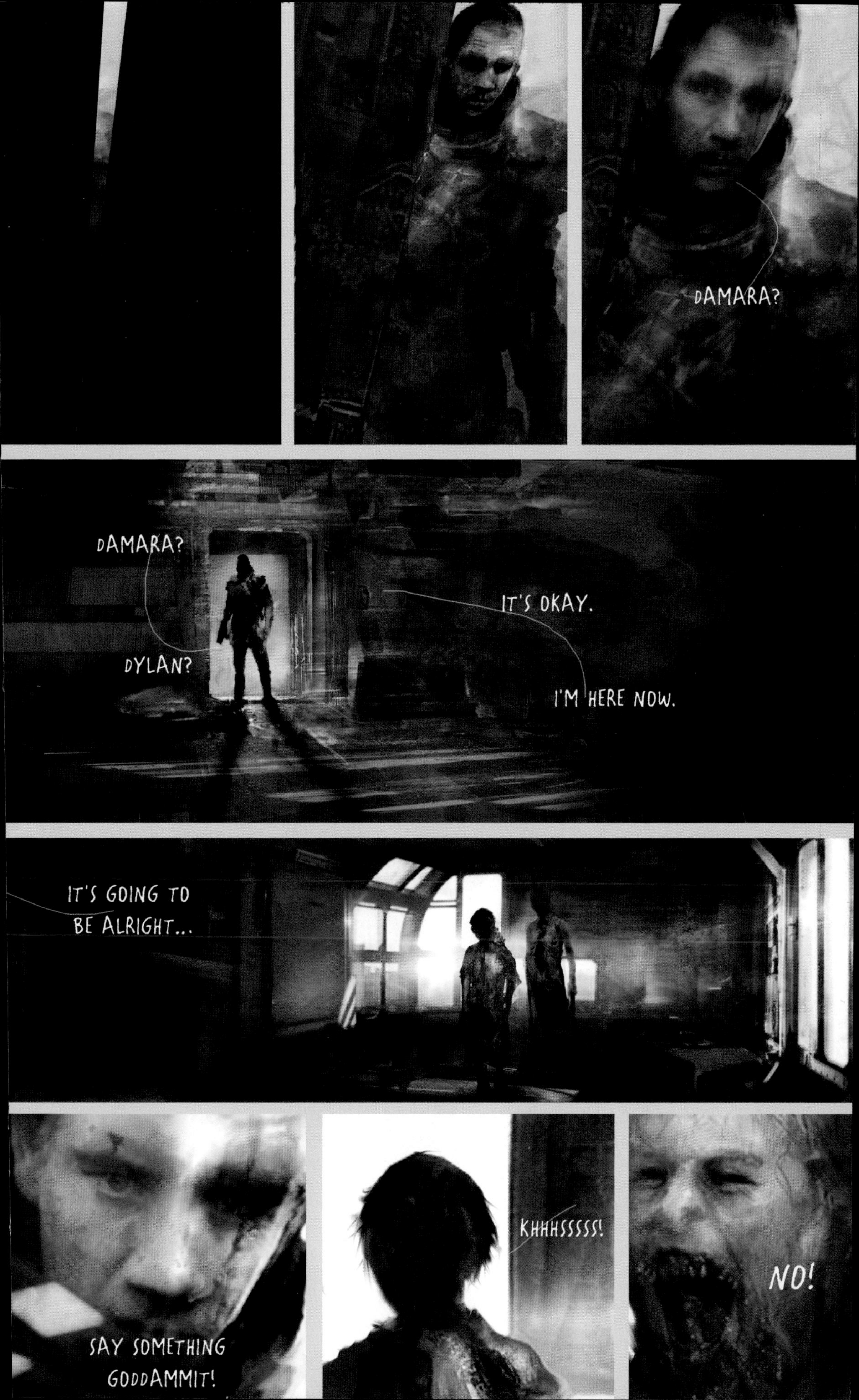
DAMARA?
DAMARA?
DYLAN?
IT'S OKAY.
I'M HERE NOW.
IT'S GOING TO BE ALRIGHT...
SAY SOMETHING GODDAMMIT!
KHHHSSSSS!
NO!

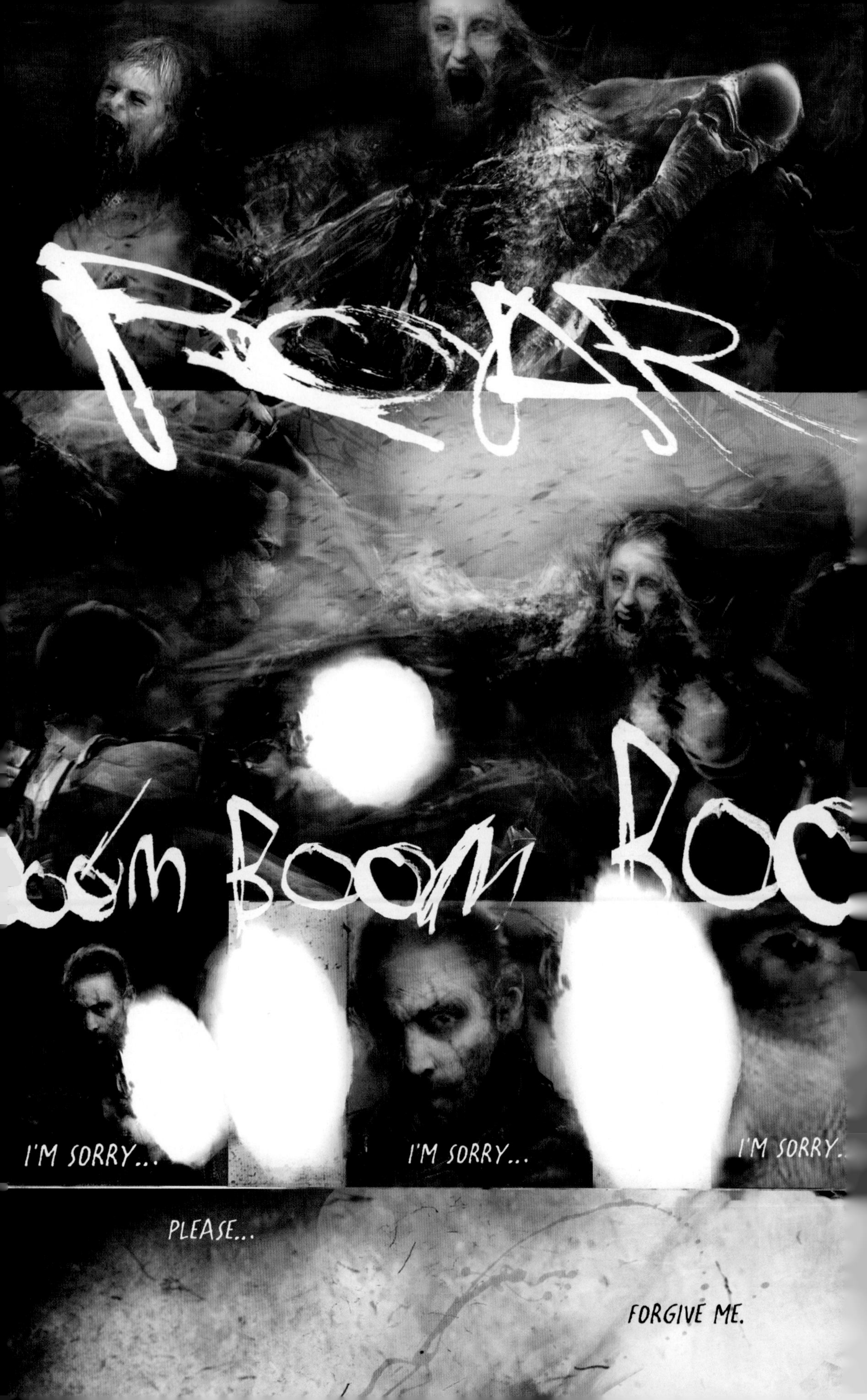
ROAR
BOOM
I'M SORRY...
I'M SORRY...
I'M SORRY...
PLEASE...
FORGIVE ME.

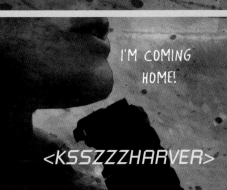

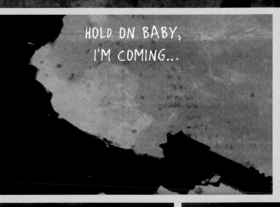

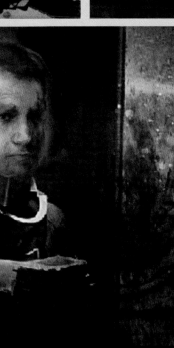

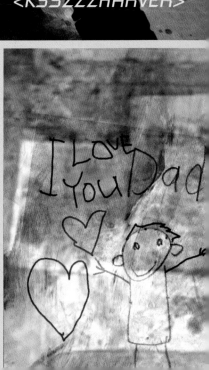

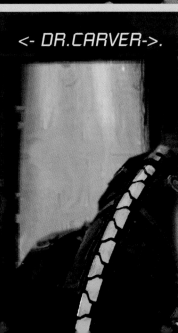

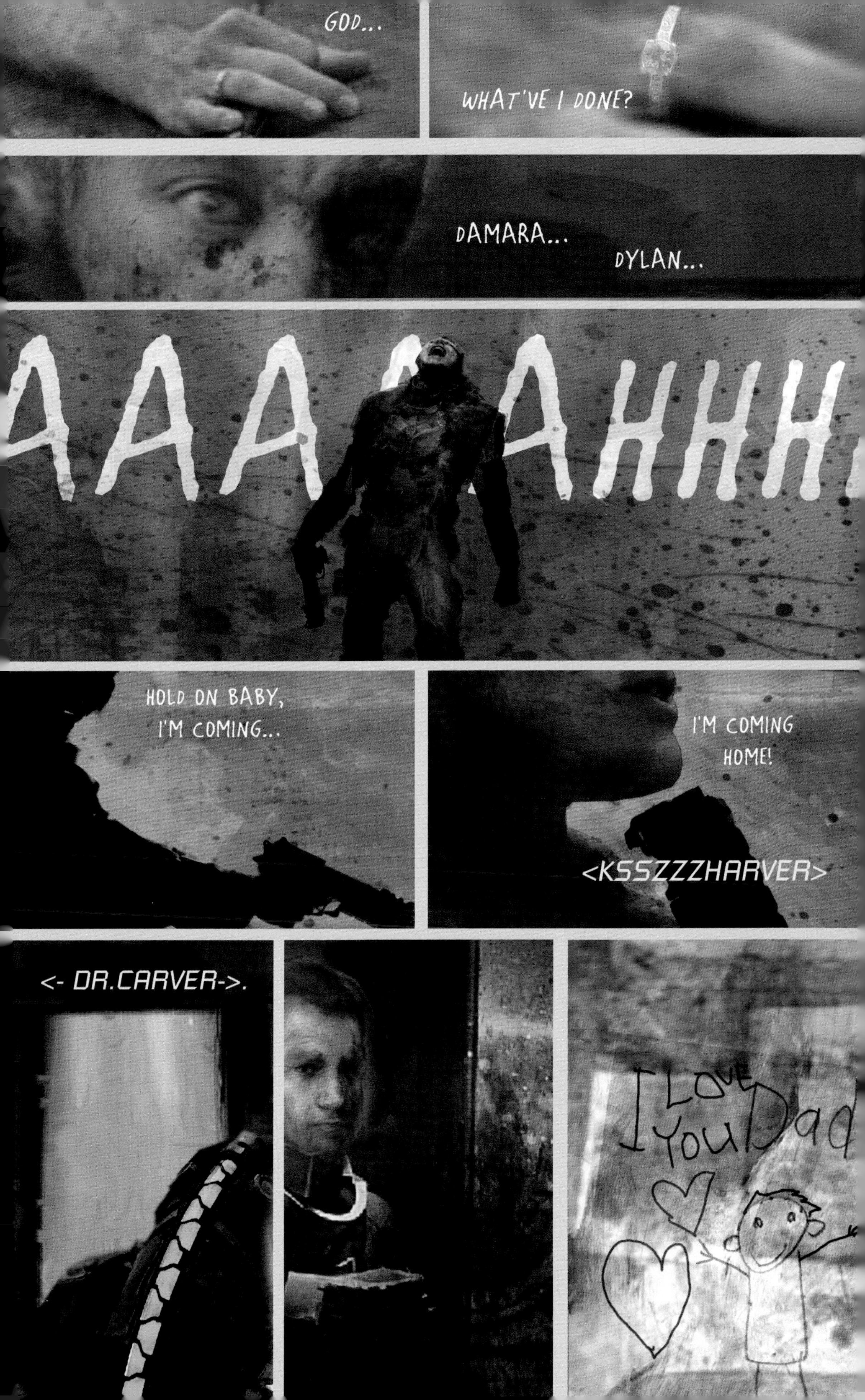
GOD...
WHAT'VE I DONE?
DAMARA...
DYLAN...
AAAAAHHH!
HOLD ON BABY, I'M COMING...
I'M COMING HOME!
<KSSZZZHARVER>
<- DR.CARVER->.
I LOVE YOU DAD

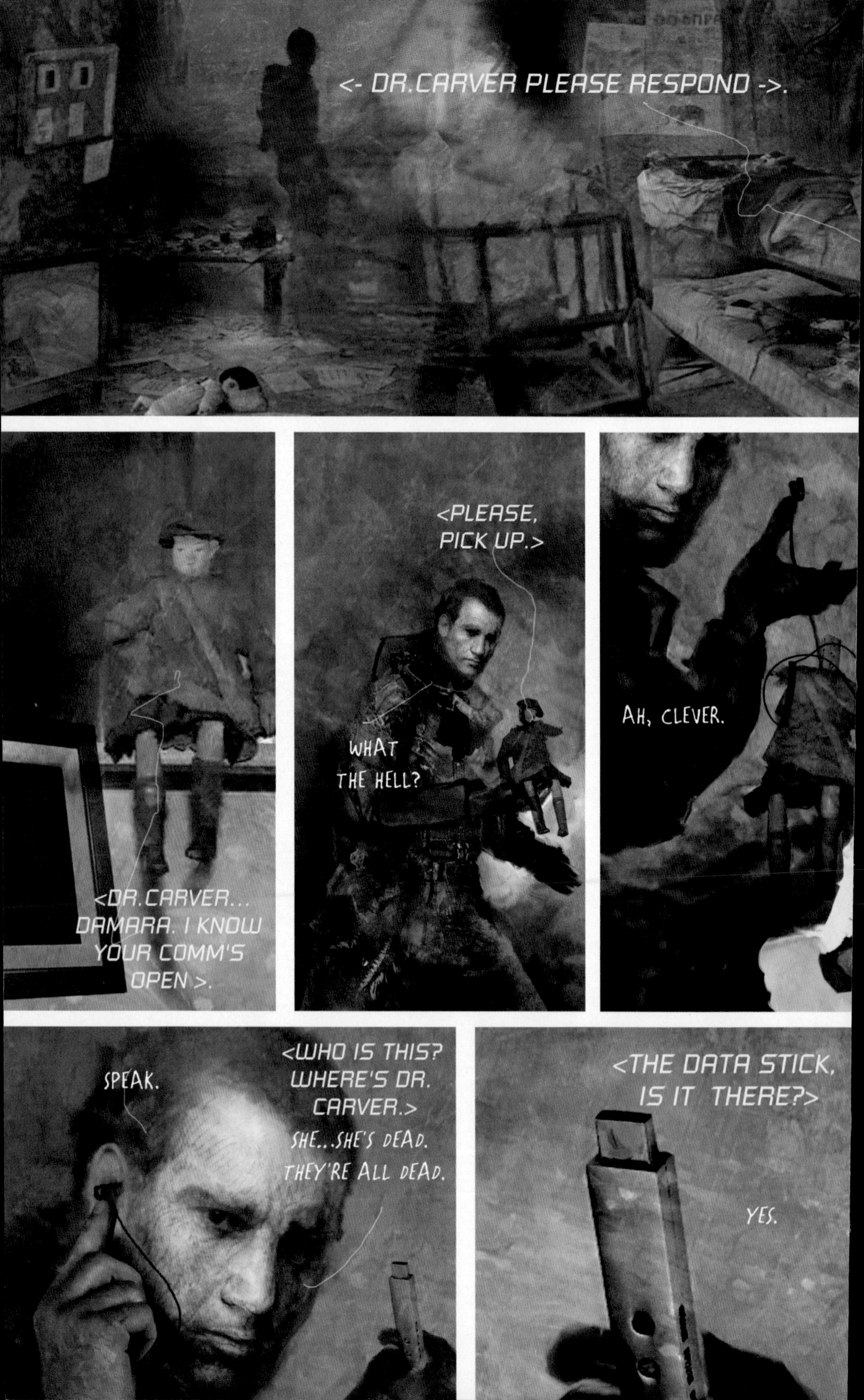
<- DR.CARVER PLEASE RESPOND ->.
<DR.CARVER... DAMARA. I KNOW YOUR COMM'S OPEN >.
<PLEASE, PICK UP.>
WHAT THE HELL?
AH, CLEVER.
SPEAK.
<WHO IS THIS? WHERE'S DR. CARVER.>
SHE...SHE'S DEAD. THEY'RE ALL DEAD.
<THE DATA STICK, IS IT THERE?>
YES.

<WAIT. GOD! JOHN? JOHN CARVER, IS THAT YOU?>

WHO WANTS TO KNOW?

<IT'S ELLIE LANGFORD.>

<I'M HERE WITH CAPTAIN ROBERT NORTON. YOU WERE STATIONED TOGETHER AT HAVEN PRIME.>

<I MET YOU AT A PARTY. MY BIRTHDAY.>

<DAMARA HAD JUST FOUND OUT SHE WAS PREGNANT WITH DYLAN.>

ELLIE...?

IS IT REALLY YOU?

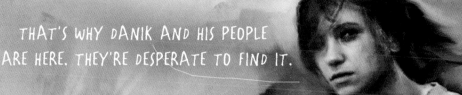

<WHAT'RE YOU DOING HERE?>

DAMARA CONTACTED ME. IN HER MARKER RESEARCH, SHE'D FOUND SOMETHING UNEXPECTED. SHE DISCOVERED THAT MARKER TAMPERING WENT WAY BACK, PAST EARTH-GOV TO THE OLD SOVEREIGN COLONIES ADMINISTRATION.

SHE WAS INVESTIGATING A MASSIVE HISTORICAL COVER-UP.

SHE'D AMASSED A GOLDMINE OF SECRETS.

THAT'S WHY DANIK AND HIS PEOPLE ARE HERE. THEY'RE DESPERATE TO FIND IT.

YEAH, I NOTICED.

WE'VE GOTTA GET OFF-WORLD. EXCEPT THE E.M.P'S TRASHED ANYTHING AIRWORTHY.

NOT A PROBLEM. ROBERT'S SHIP, THE EUDORA'S IN HIGH ORBIT.

HE CAN COME GET US.

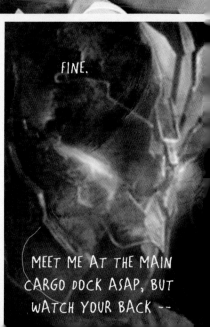

FINE.

MEET ME AT THE MAIN CARGO DOCK ASAP, BUT WATCH YOUR BACK --

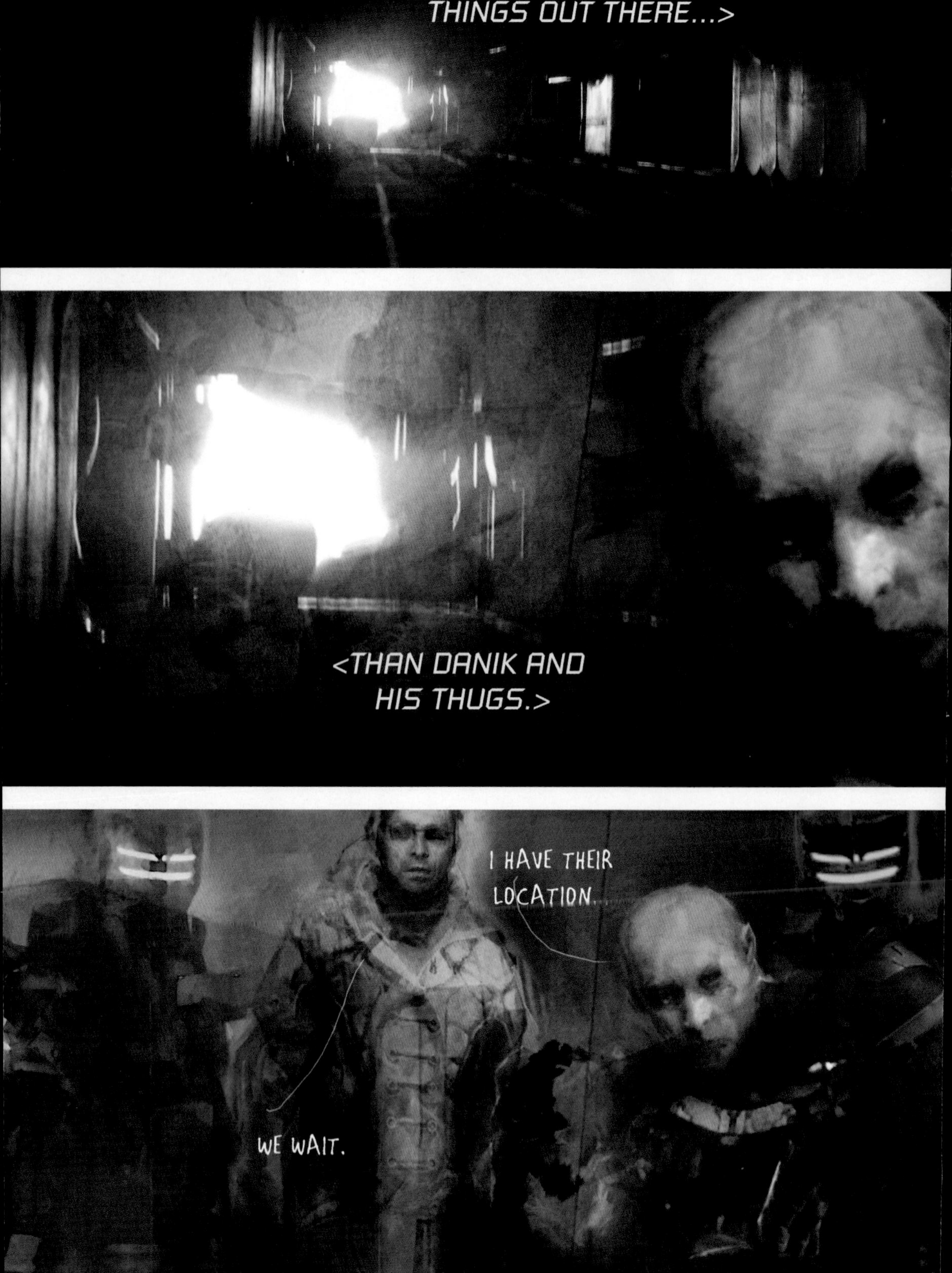
THINGS OUT THERE...>
<THAN DANIK AND HIS THUGS.>
I HAVE THEIR LOCATION...
WE WAIT.

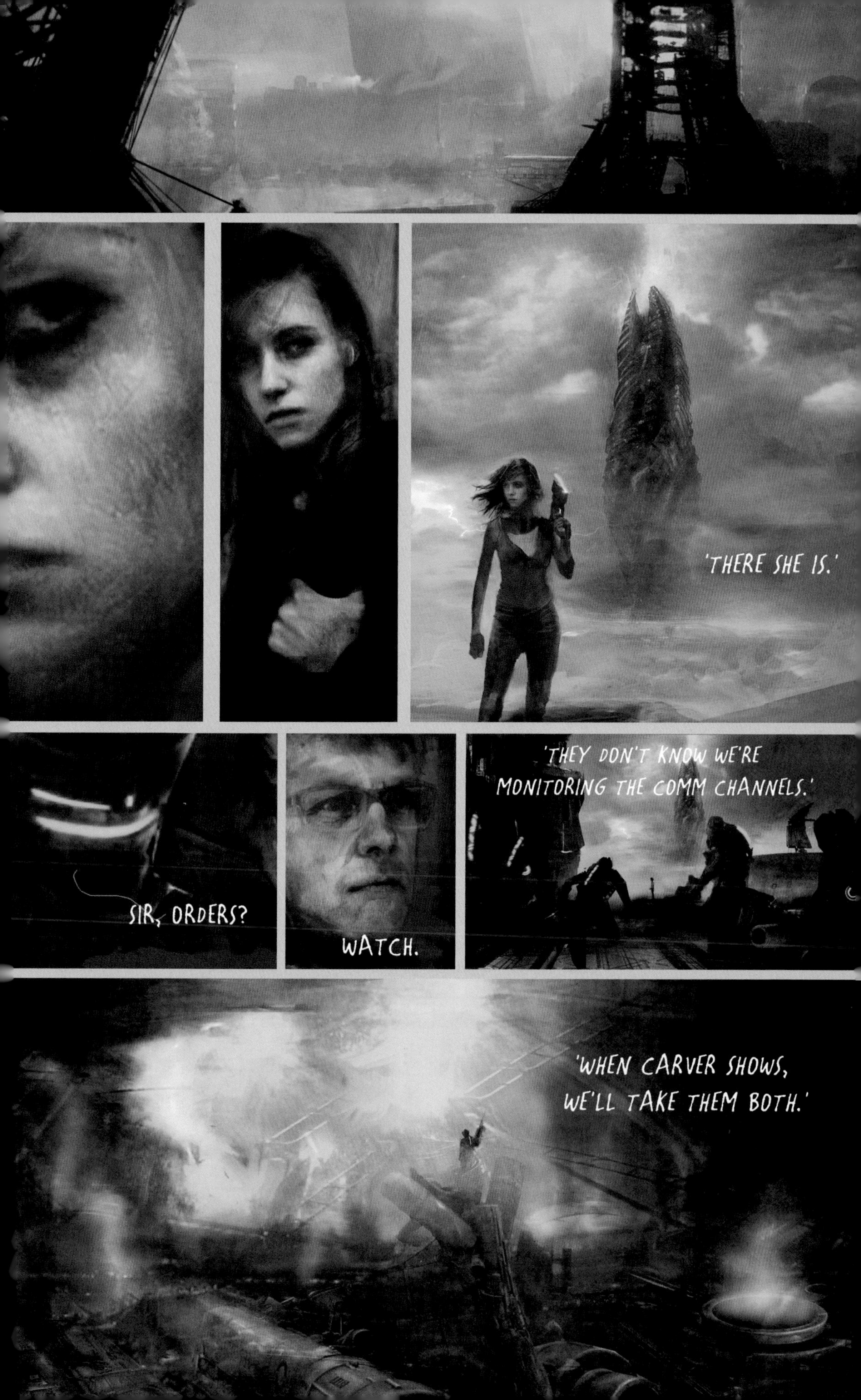
'THERE SHE IS.'
SIR, ORDERS?
WATCH.
'THEY DON'T KNOW WE'RE MONITORING THE COMM CHANNELS.'
'WHEN CARVER SHOWS, WE'LL TAKE THEM BOTH.'

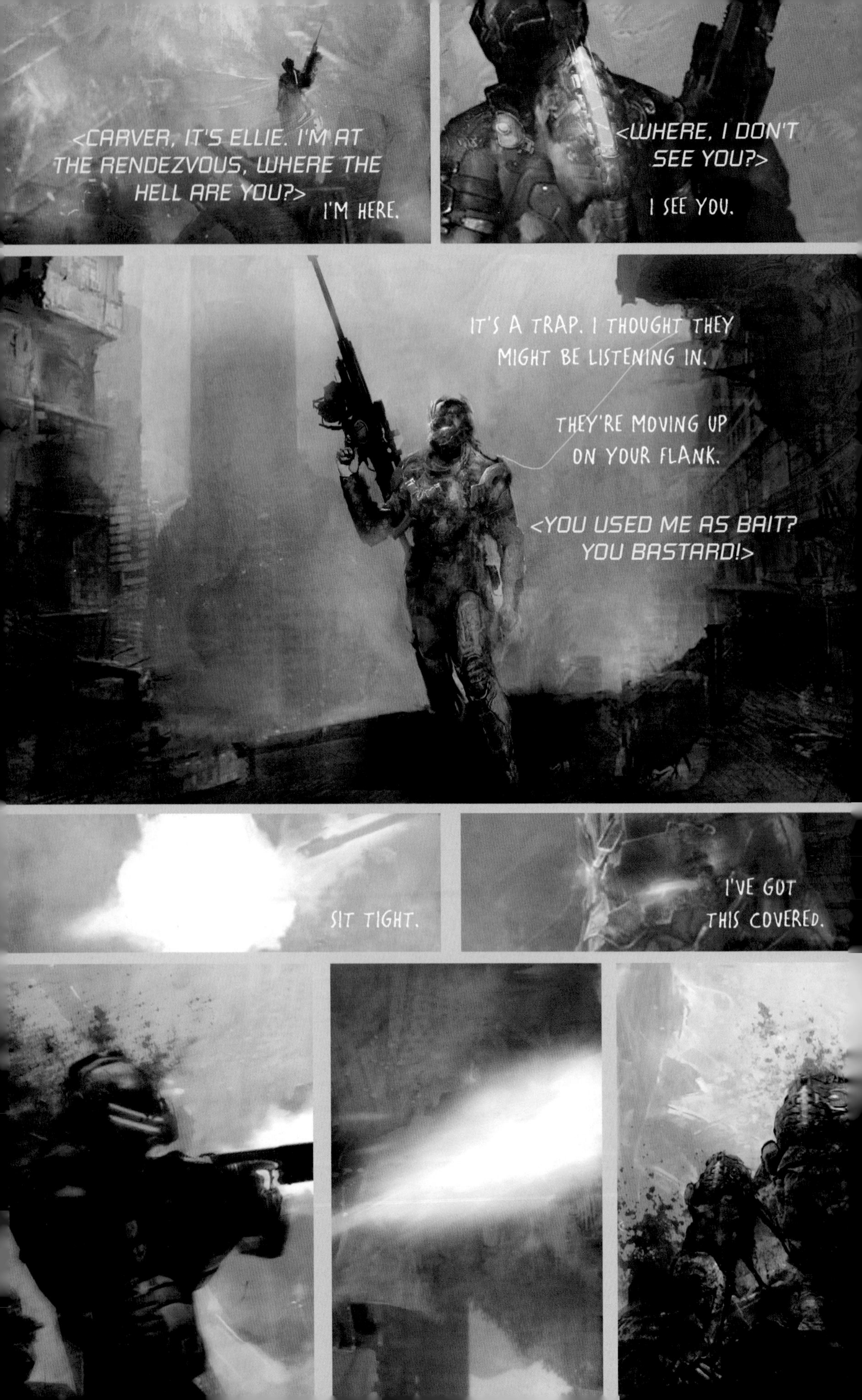
<CARVER, IT'S ELLIE. I'M AT THE RENDEZVOUS, WHERE THE HELL ARE YOU?>
I'M HERE.
<WHERE, I DON'T SEE YOU?>
I SEE YOU.
IT'S A TRAP. I THOUGHT THEY MIGHT BE LISTENING IN.
THEY'RE MOVING UP ON YOUR FLANK.
<YOU USED ME AS BAIT? YOU BASTARD!>
SIT TIGHT.
I'VE GOT THIS COVERED.

ELLIE—

GET READY TO MOVE OUT!

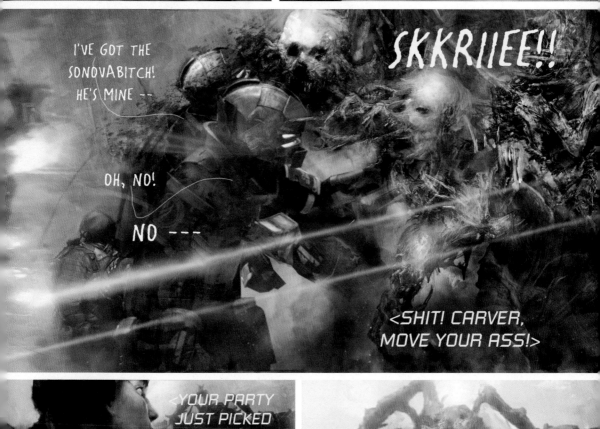

I'VE GOT THE SONOVABITCH! HE'S MINE --

SKKRIIEE!!

OH, NO!

NO ---

<SHIT! CARVER, MOVE YOUR ASS!>

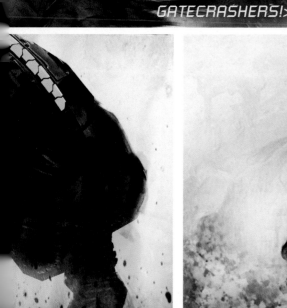

<YOUR PARTY JUST PICKED UP SOME GATECRASHERS!>

I'M ON MY WAY!

IT'S THE EUDORA!

LOOKS TO ME LIKE
THE ODDS JUST
CHANGED!

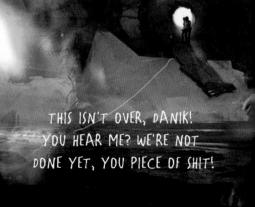

THIS ISN'T OVER, DANIK!
YOU HEAR ME? WE'RE NOT
DONE YET, YOU PIECE OF SHIT!

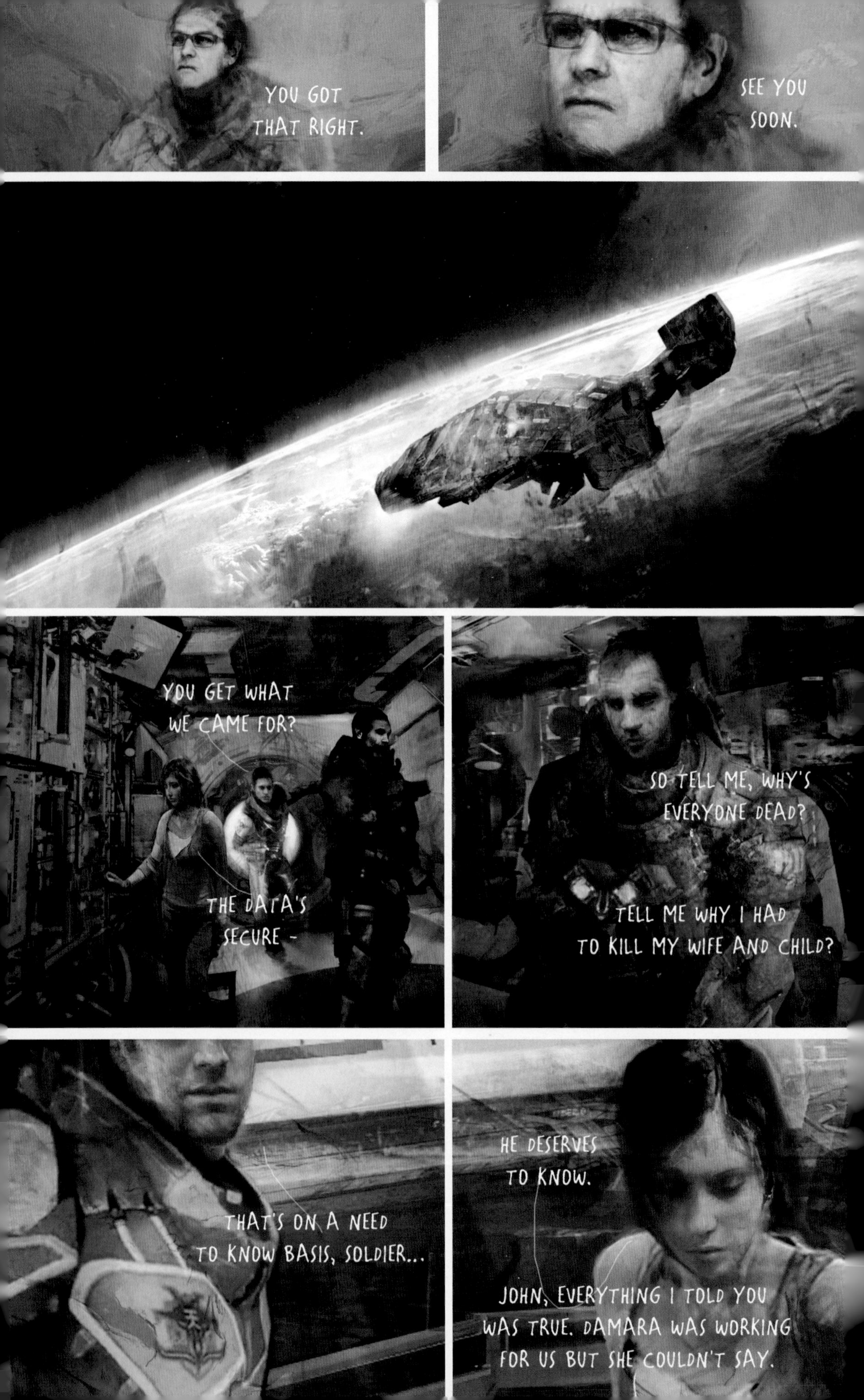
YOU GOT THAT RIGHT.
SEE YOU SOON.
YOU GET WHAT WE CAME FOR?
THE DATA'S SECURE -
SO TELL ME, WHY'S EVERYONE DEAD?
TELL ME WHY I HAD TO KILL MY WIFE AND CHILD?
THAT'S ON A NEED TO KNOW BASIS, SOLDIER...
HE DESERVES TO KNOW.
JOHN, EVERYTHING I TOLD YOU WAS TRUE. DAMARA WAS WORKING FOR US BUT SHE COULDN'T SAY.

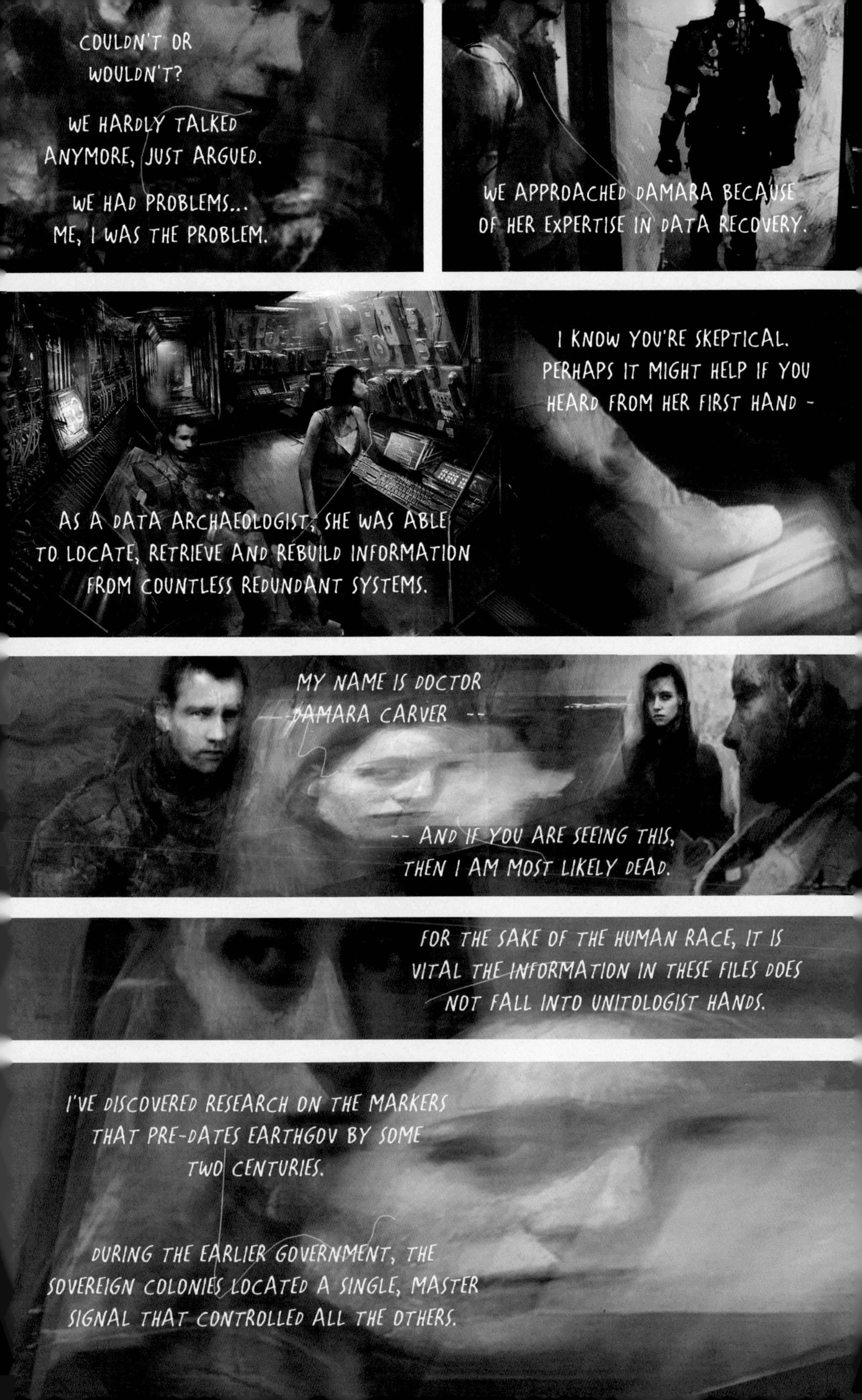
COULDN'T OR WOULDN'T?
WE HARDLY TALKED ANYMORE, JUST ARGUED.
WE HAD PROBLEMS... ME, I WAS THE PROBLEM.
WE APPROACHED DAMARA BECAUSE OF HER EXPERTISE IN DATA RECOVERY.
I KNOW YOU'RE SKEPTICAL. PERHAPS IT MIGHT HELP IF YOU HEARD FROM HER FIRST HAND -
AS A DATA ARCHAEOLOGIST, SHE WAS ABLE TO LOCATE, RETRIEVE AND REBUILD INFORMATION FROM COUNTLESS REDUNDANT SYSTEMS.
MY NAME IS DOCTOR DAMARA CARVER --
-- AND IF YOU ARE SEEING THIS, THEN I AM MOST LIKELY DEAD.
FOR THE SAKE OF THE HUMAN RACE, IT IS VITAL THE INFORMATION IN THESE FILES DOES NOT FALL INTO UNITOLOGIST HANDS.
I'VE DISCOVERED RESEARCH ON THE MARKERS THAT PRE-DATES EARTHGOV BY SOME TWO CENTURIES.
DURING THE EARLIER GOVERNMENT, THE SOVEREIGN COLONIES LOCATED A SINGLE, MASTER SIGNAL THAT CONTROLLED ALL THE OTHERS.

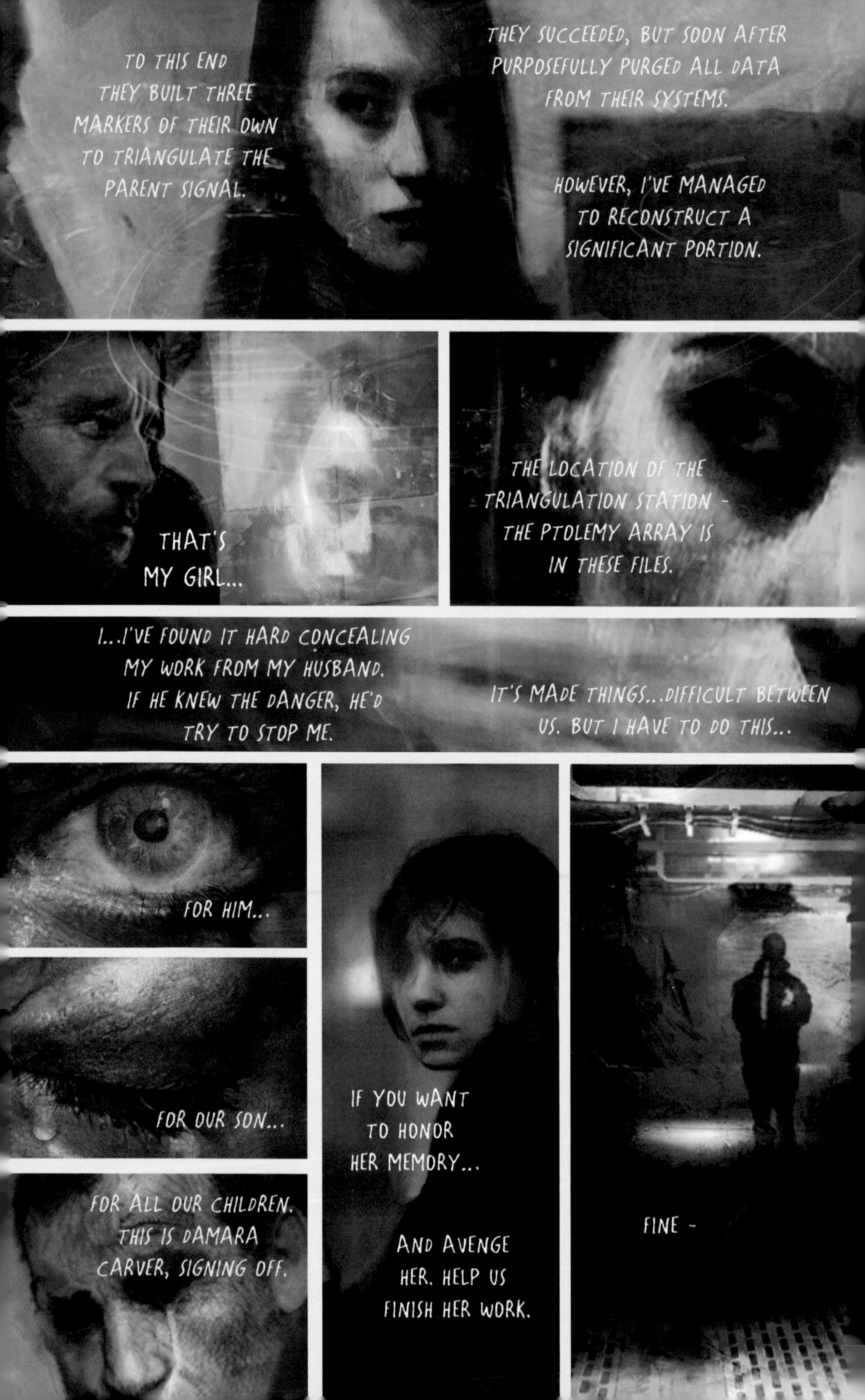

TO THIS END THEY BUILT THREE MARKERS OF THEIR OWN TO TRIANGULATE THE PARENT SIGNAL.

THEY SUCCEEDED, BUT SOON AFTER PURPOSEFULLY PURGED ALL DATA FROM THEIR SYSTEMS.

HOWEVER, I'VE MANAGED TO RECONSTRUCT A SIGNIFICANT PORTION.

THAT'S MY GIRL...

THE LOCATION OF THE TRIANGULATION STATION - THE PTOLEMY ARRAY IS IN THESE FILES.

I...I'VE FOUND IT HARD CONCEALING MY WORK FROM MY HUSBAND. IF HE KNEW THE DANGER, HE'D TRY TO STOP ME.

IT'S MADE THINGS...DIFFICULT BETWEEN US. BUT I HAVE TO DO THIS...

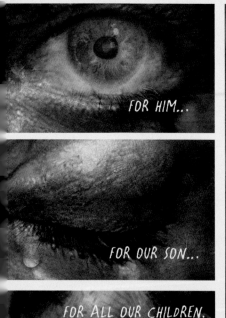

FOR HIM...

FOR OUR SON...

FOR ALL OUR CHILDREN. THIS IS DAMARA CARVER, SIGNING OFF.

IF YOU WANT TO HONOR HER MEMORY...

AND AVENGE HER. HELP US FINISH HER WORK.

FINE -

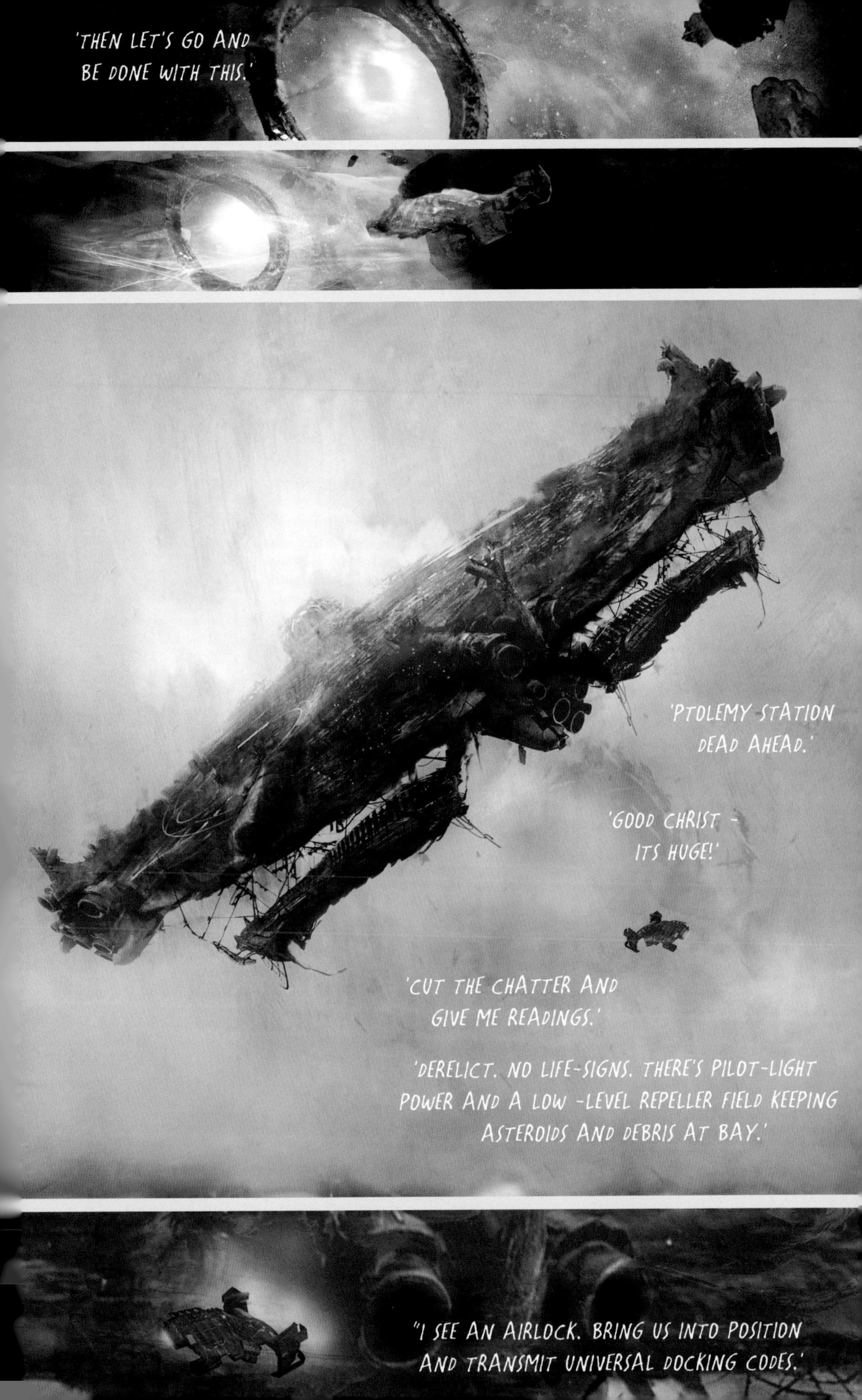
'THEN LET'S GO AND BE DONE WITH THIS.'
'PTOLEMY STATION DEAD AHEAD.'
'GOOD CHRIST – ITS HUGE!'
'CUT THE CHATTER AND GIVE ME READINGS.'
'DERELICT. NO LIFE-SIGNS. THERE'S PILOT-LIGHT POWER AND A LOW -LEVEL REPELLER FIELD KEEPING ASTEROIDS AND DEBRIS AT BAY.'
'I SEE AN AIRLOCK. BRING US INTO POSITION AND TRANSMIT UNIVERSAL DOCKING CODES.'

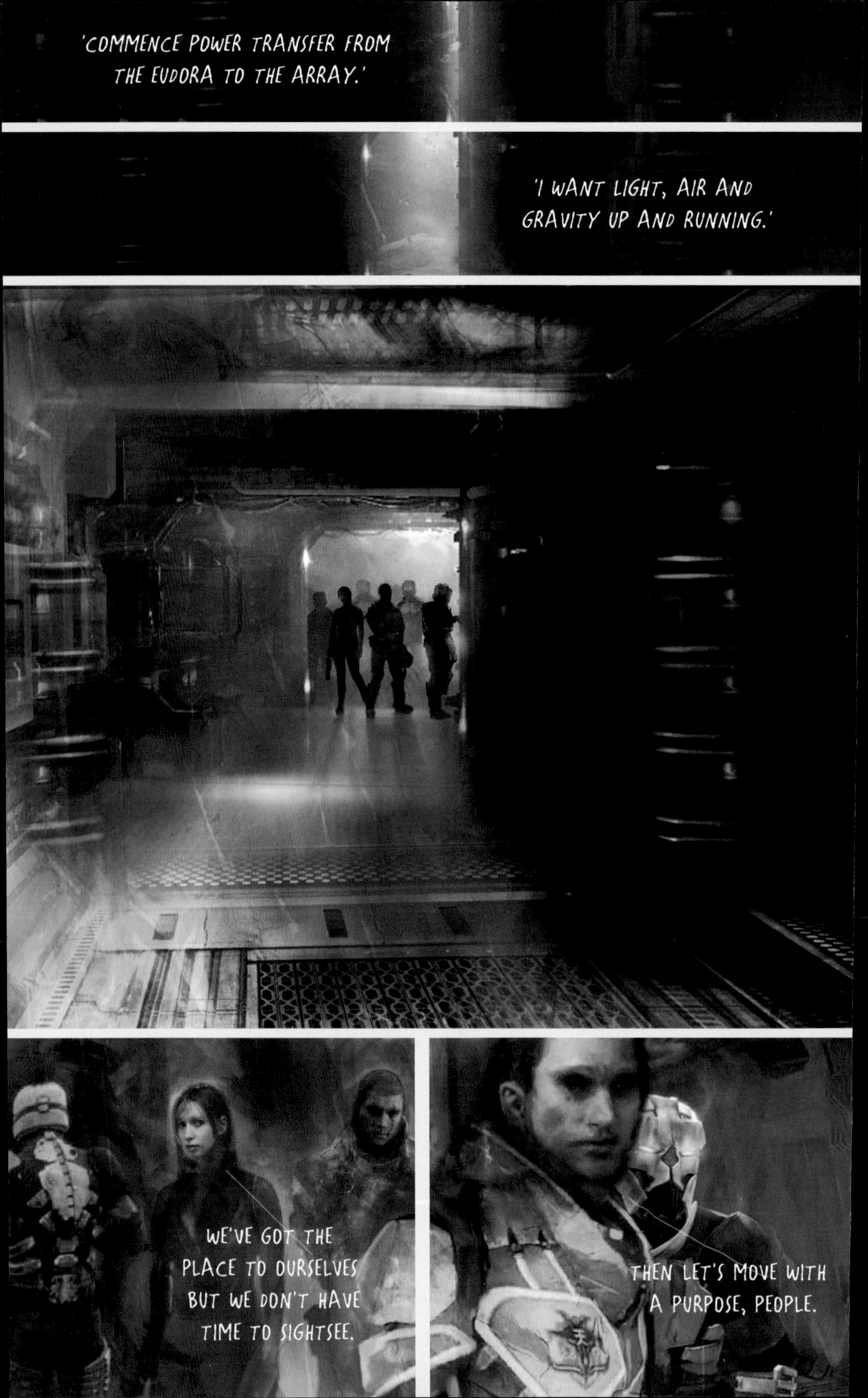
'COMMENCE POWER TRANSFER FROM THE EUDORA TO THE ARRAY.'
'I WANT LIGHT, AIR AND GRAVITY UP AND RUNNING.'
WE'VE GOT THE PLACE TO OURSELVES BUT WE DON'T HAVE TIME TO SIGHTSEE.
THEN LET'S MOVE WITH A PURPOSE, PEOPLE.

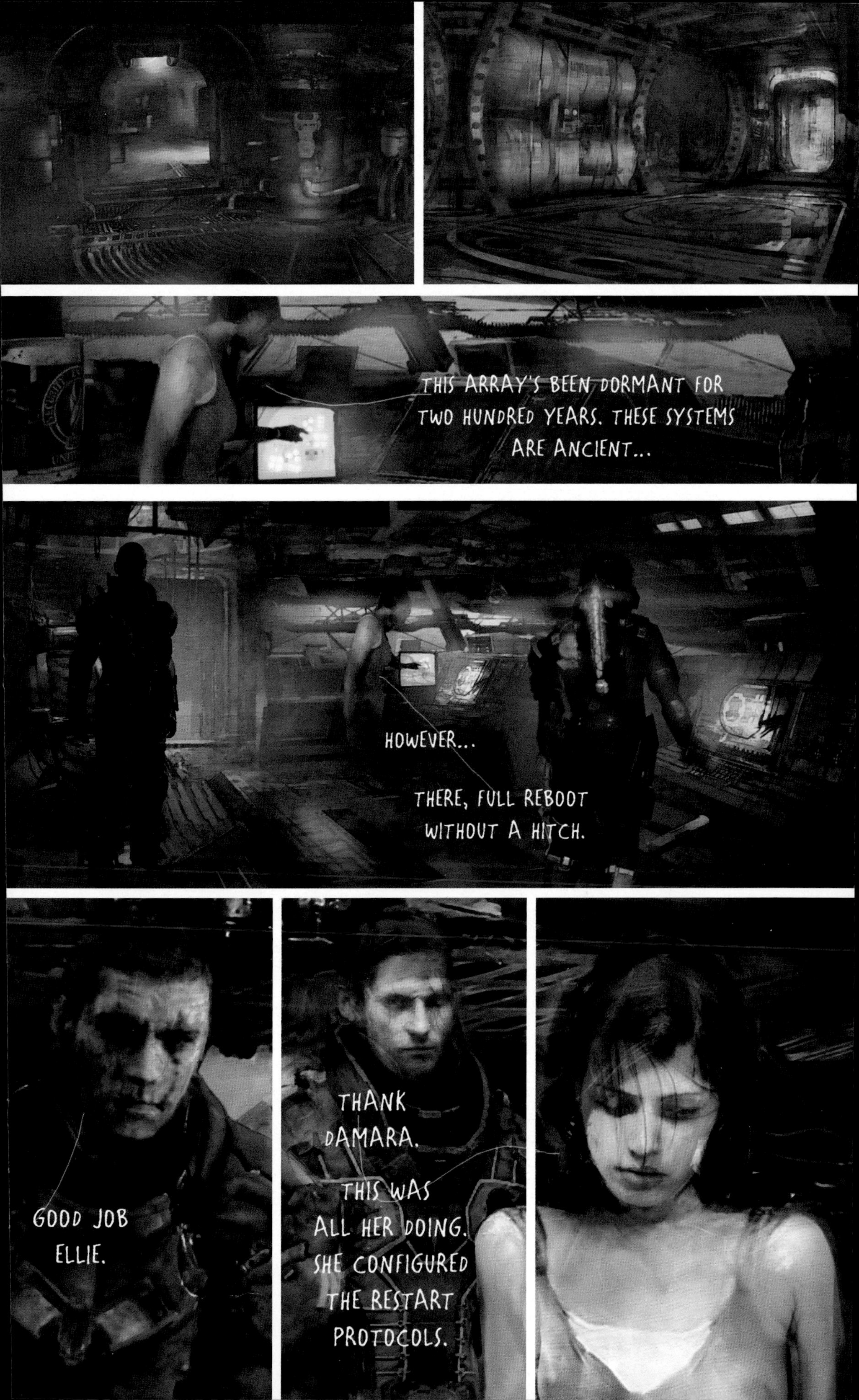
THIS ARRAY'S BEEN DORMANT FOR TWO HUNDRED YEARS. THESE SYSTEMS ARE ANCIENT...
HOWEVER...
THERE, FULL REBOOT WITHOUT A HITCH.
GOOD JOB ELLIE.
THANK DAMARA.
THIS WAS ALL HER DOING. SHE CONFIGURED THE RESTART PROTOCOLS.

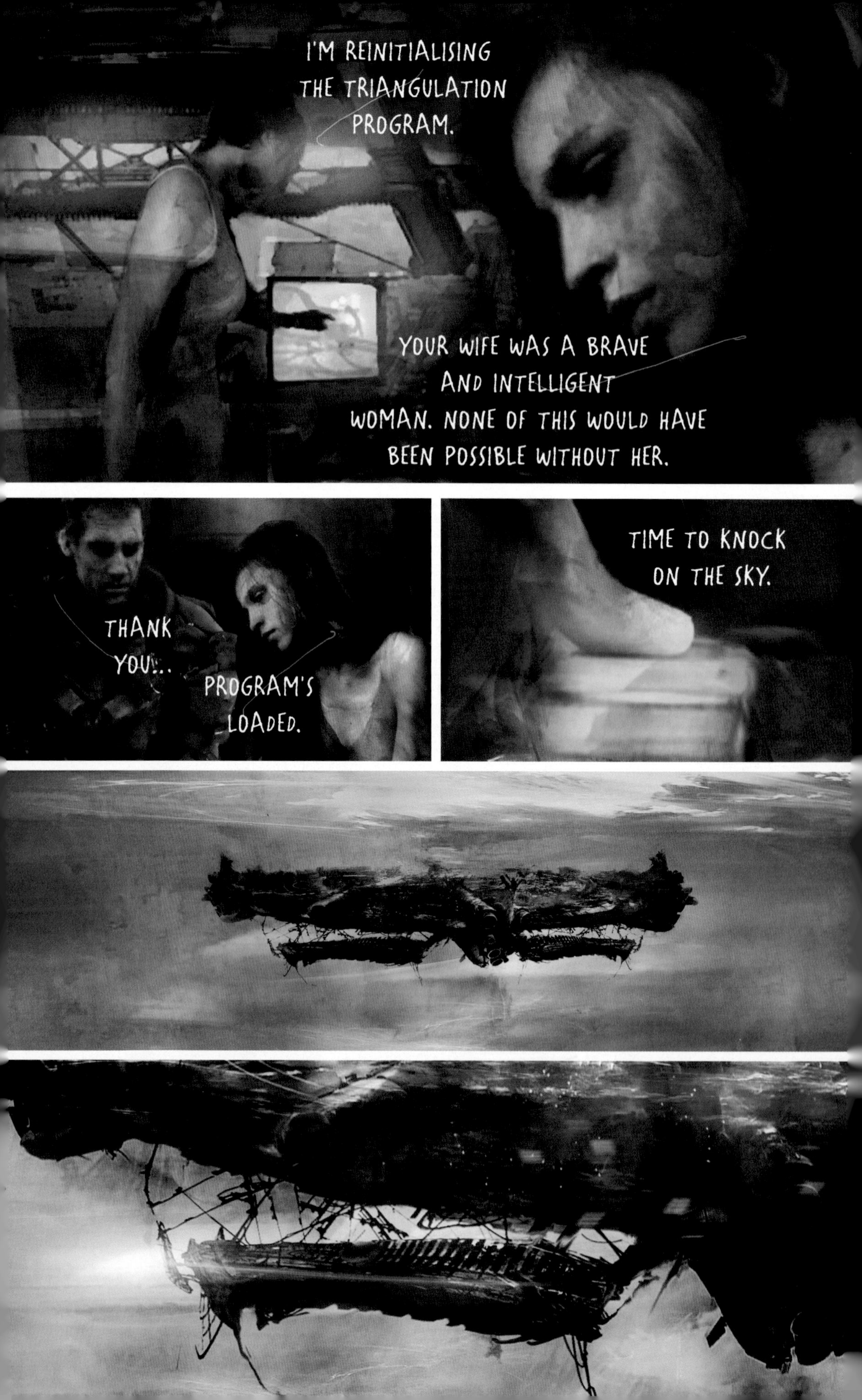
I'M REINITIALISING THE TRIANGULATION PROGRAM.
YOUR WIFE WAS A BRAVE AND INTELLIGENT WOMAN. NONE OF THIS WOULD HAVE BEEN POSSIBLE WITHOUT HER.
THANK YOU...
PROGRAM'S LOADED.
TIME TO KNOCK ON THE SKY.

'MARKER PYLONS DEPLOYED.'

'MARKERS EXPOSED AND CHARGING.'

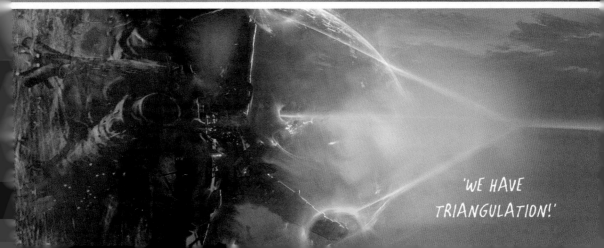

'WE HAVE TRIANGULATION!'

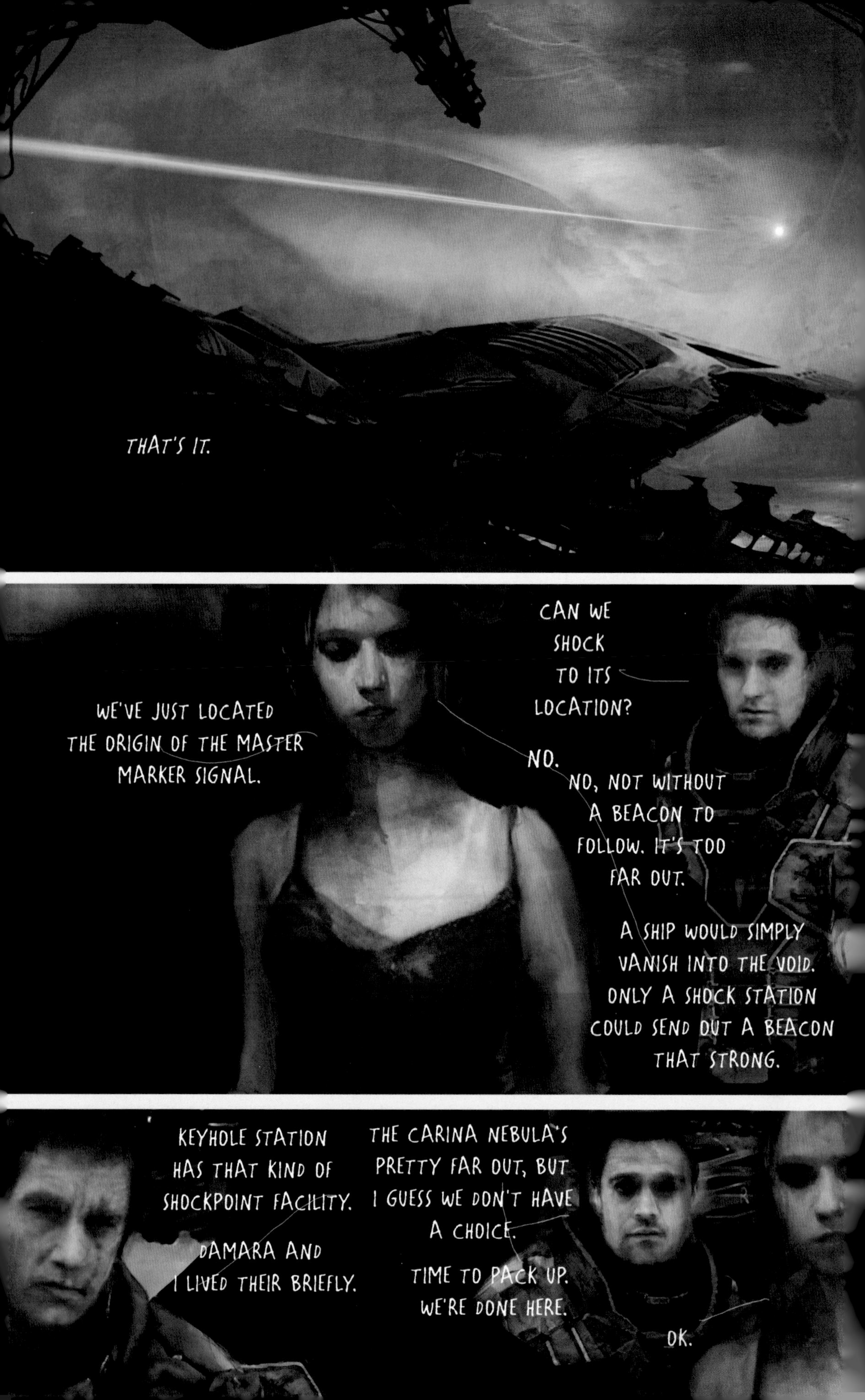
THAT'S IT.
WE'VE JUST LOCATED THE ORIGIN OF THE MASTER MARKER SIGNAL.
CAN WE SHOCK TO ITS LOCATION?
NO.
NO, NOT WITHOUT A BEACON TO FOLLOW. IT'S TOO FAR OUT.
A SHIP WOULD SIMPLY VANISH INTO THE VOID. ONLY A SHOCK STATION COULD SEND OUT A BEACON THAT STRONG.
KEYHOLE STATION HAS THAT KIND OF SHOCKPOINT FACILITY.
DAMARA AND I LIVED THEIR BRIEFLY.
THE CARINA NEBULA'S PRETTY FAR OUT, BUT I GUESS WE DON'T HAVE A CHOICE.
TIME TO PACK UP. WE'RE DONE HERE.
OK.

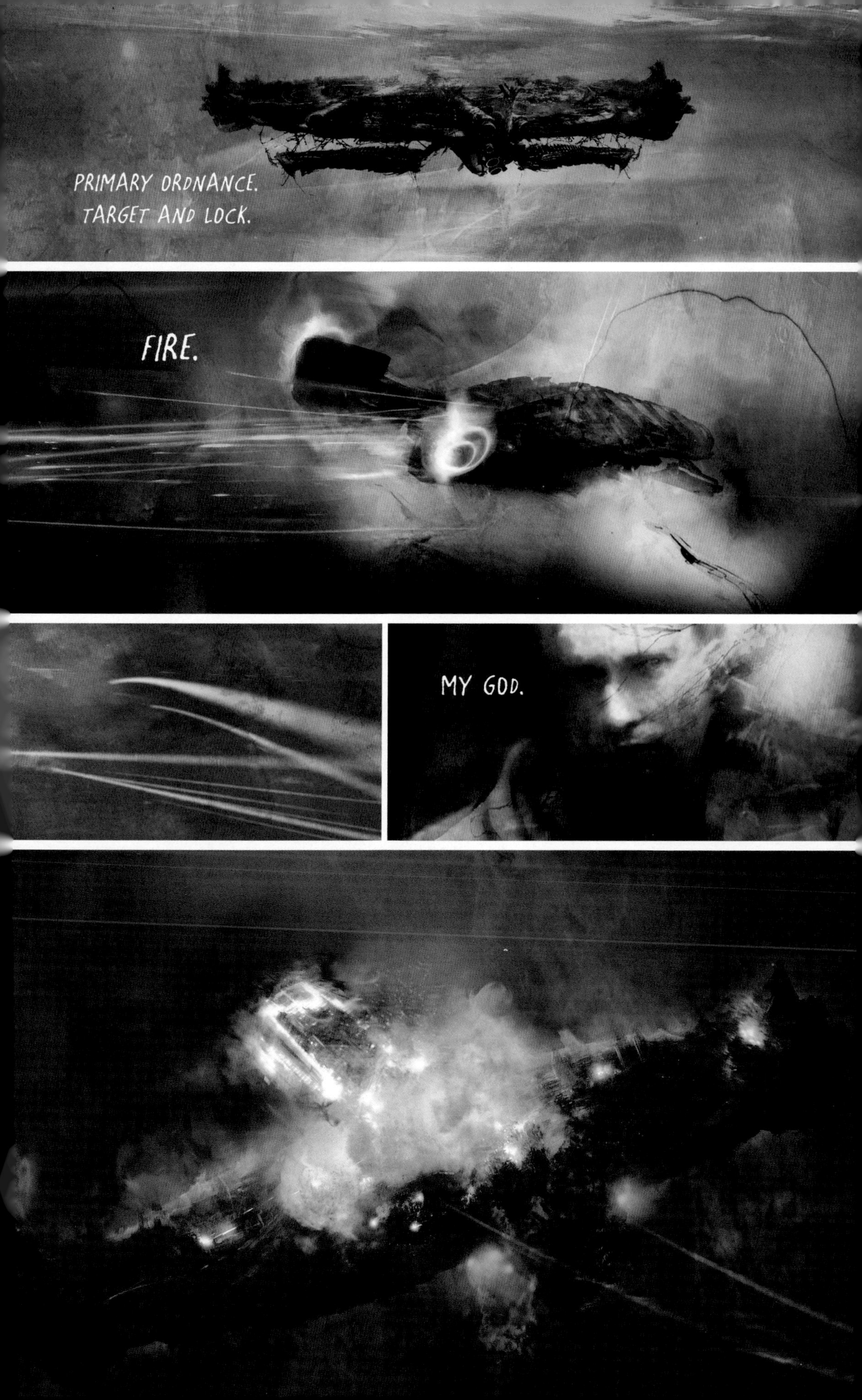
PRIMARY ORDNANCE. TARGET AND LOCK.
FIRE.
MY GOD.

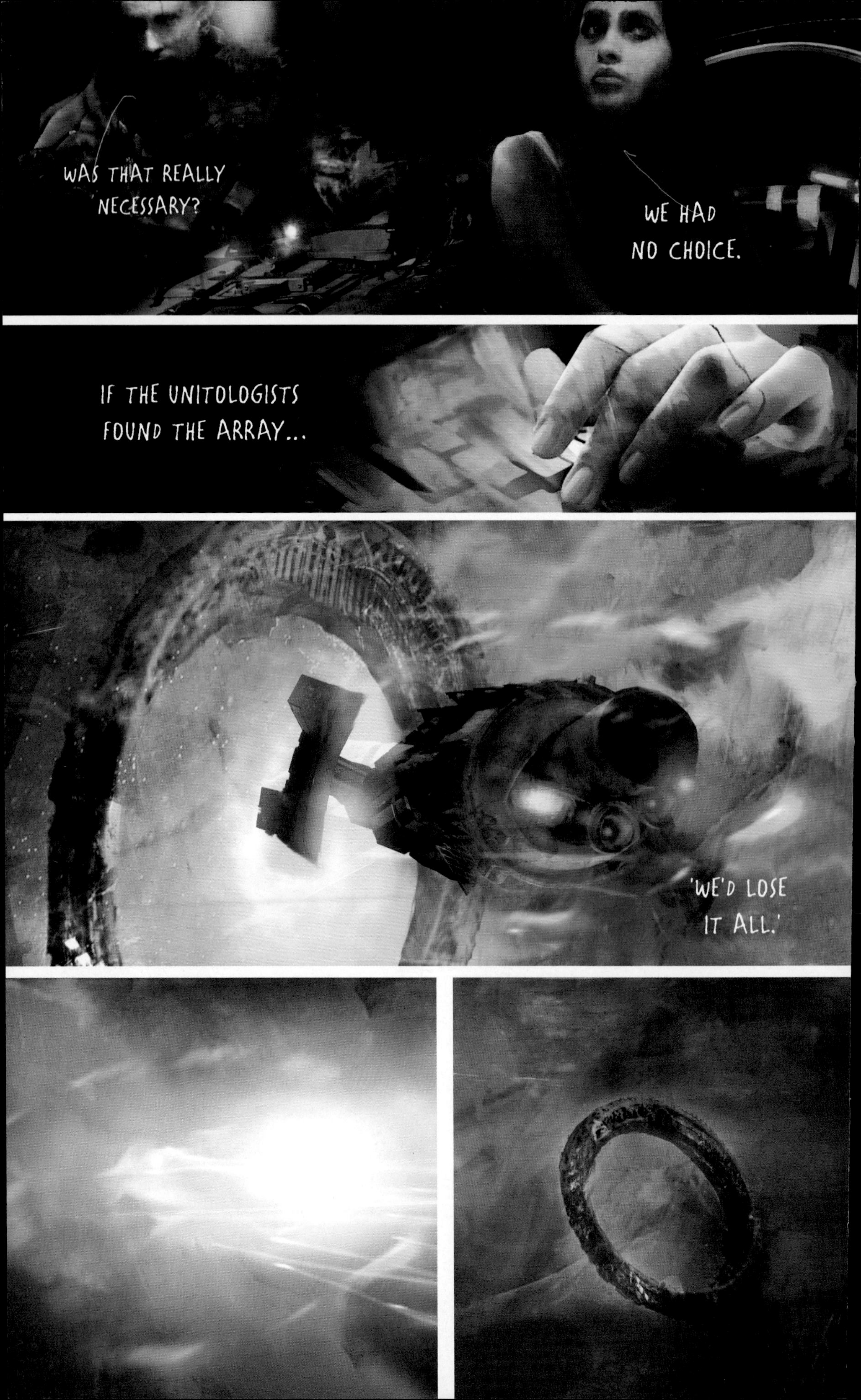
WAS THAT REALLY NECESSARY?
WE HAD NO CHOICE.
IF THE UNITOLOGISTS FOUND THE ARRAY...
'WE'D LOSE IT ALL.'

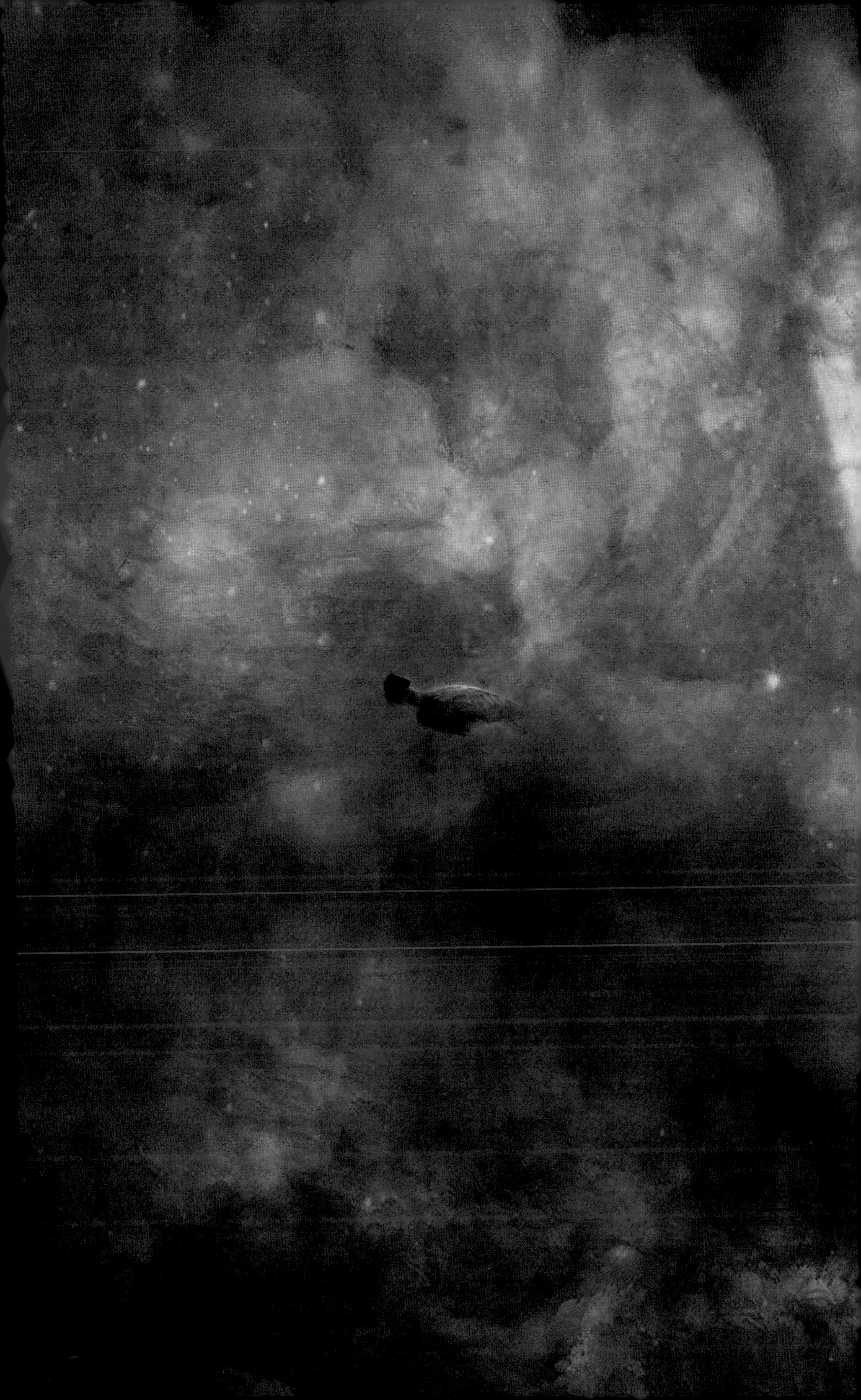

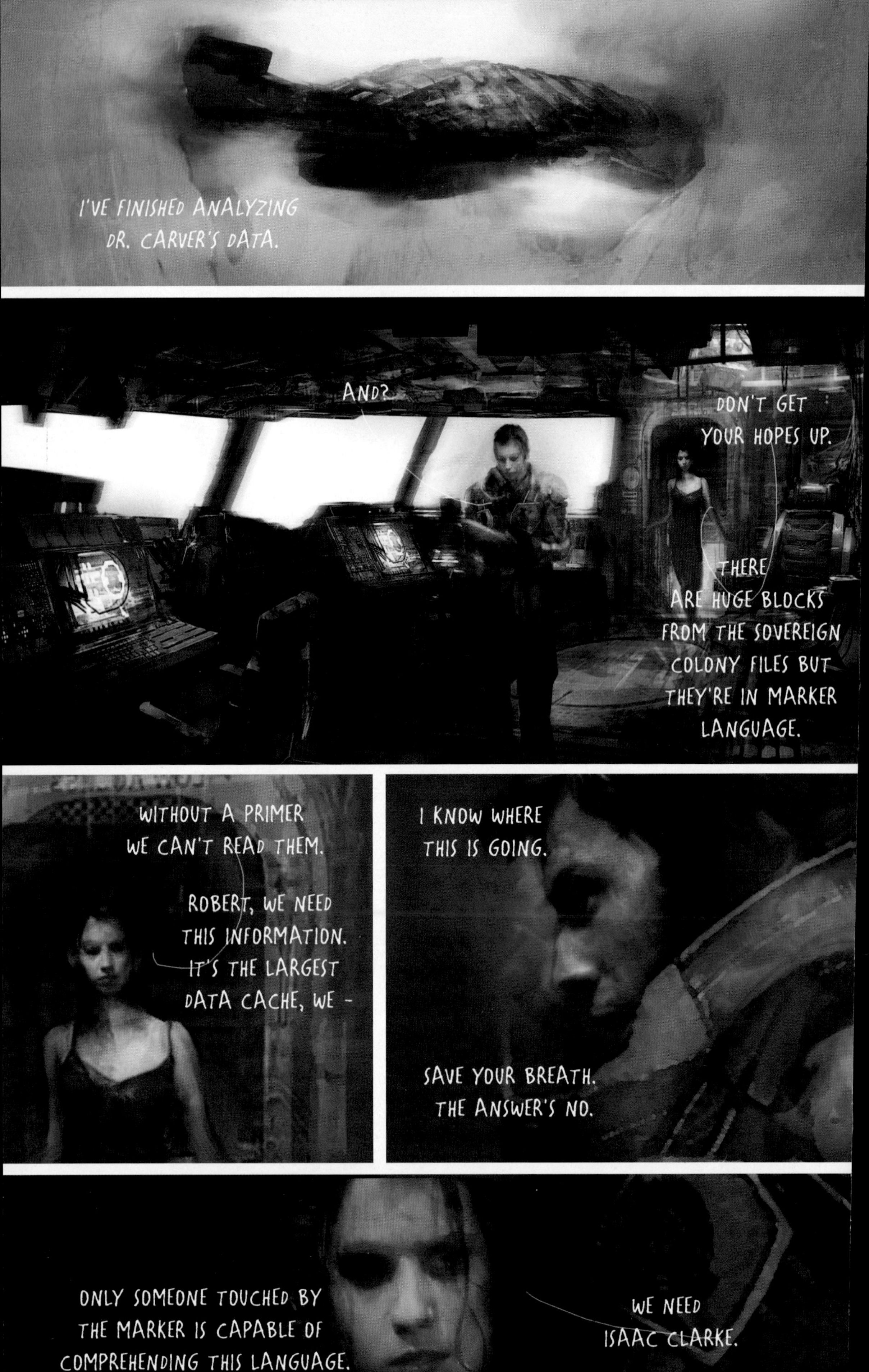
I'VE FINISHED ANALYZING DR. CARVER'S DATA.
AND?
DON'T GET YOUR HOPES UP.
THERE ARE HUGE BLOCKS FROM THE SOVEREIGN COLONY FILES BUT THEY'RE IN MARKER LANGUAGE.
WITHOUT A PRIMER WE CAN'T READ THEM.
ROBERT, WE NEED THIS INFORMATION. IT'S THE LARGEST DATA CACHE, WE -
I KNOW WHERE THIS IS GOING.
SAVE YOUR BREATH. THE ANSWER'S NO.
ONLY SOMEONE TOUCHED BY THE MARKER IS CAPABLE OF COMPREHENDING THIS LANGUAGE.
WE NEED ISAAC CLARKE.

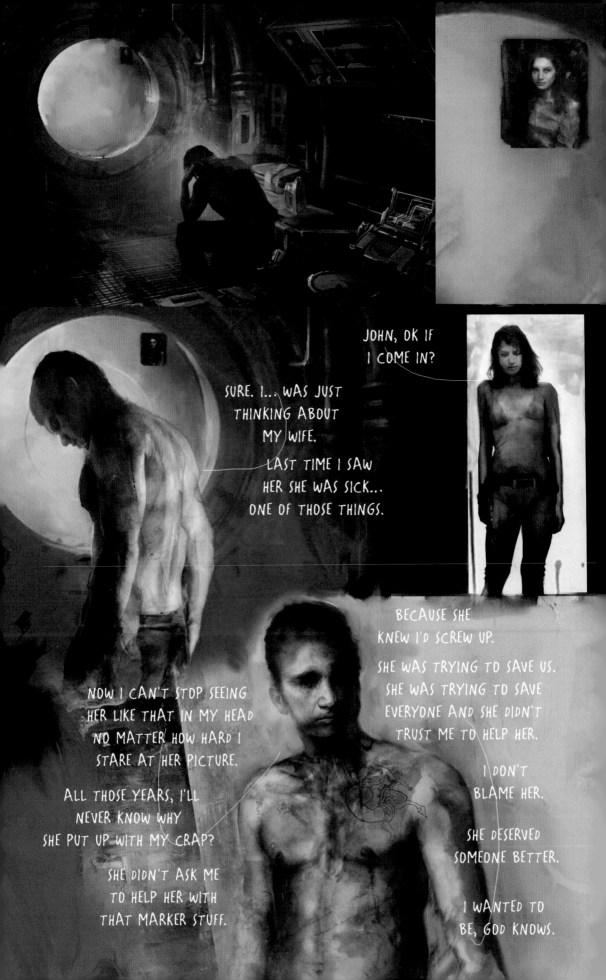

JOHN, OK IF I COME IN?

SURE. I... WAS JUST THINKING ABOUT MY WIFE.

LAST TIME I SAW HER SHE WAS SICK... ONE OF THOSE THINGS.

BECAUSE SHE KNEW I'D SCREW UP.

SHE WAS TRYING TO SAVE US. SHE WAS TRYING TO SAVE EVERYONE AND SHE DIDN'T TRUST ME TO HELP HER.

NOW I CAN'T STOP SEEING HER LIKE THAT IN MY HEAD NO MATTER HOW HARD I STARE AT HER PICTURE.

I DON'T BLAME HER.

ALL THOSE YEARS, I'LL NEVER KNOW WHY SHE PUT UP WITH MY CRAP?

SHE DESERVED SOMEONE BETTER.

SHE DIDN'T ASK ME TO HELP HER WITH THAT MARKER STUFF.

I WANTED TO BE, GOD KNOWS.

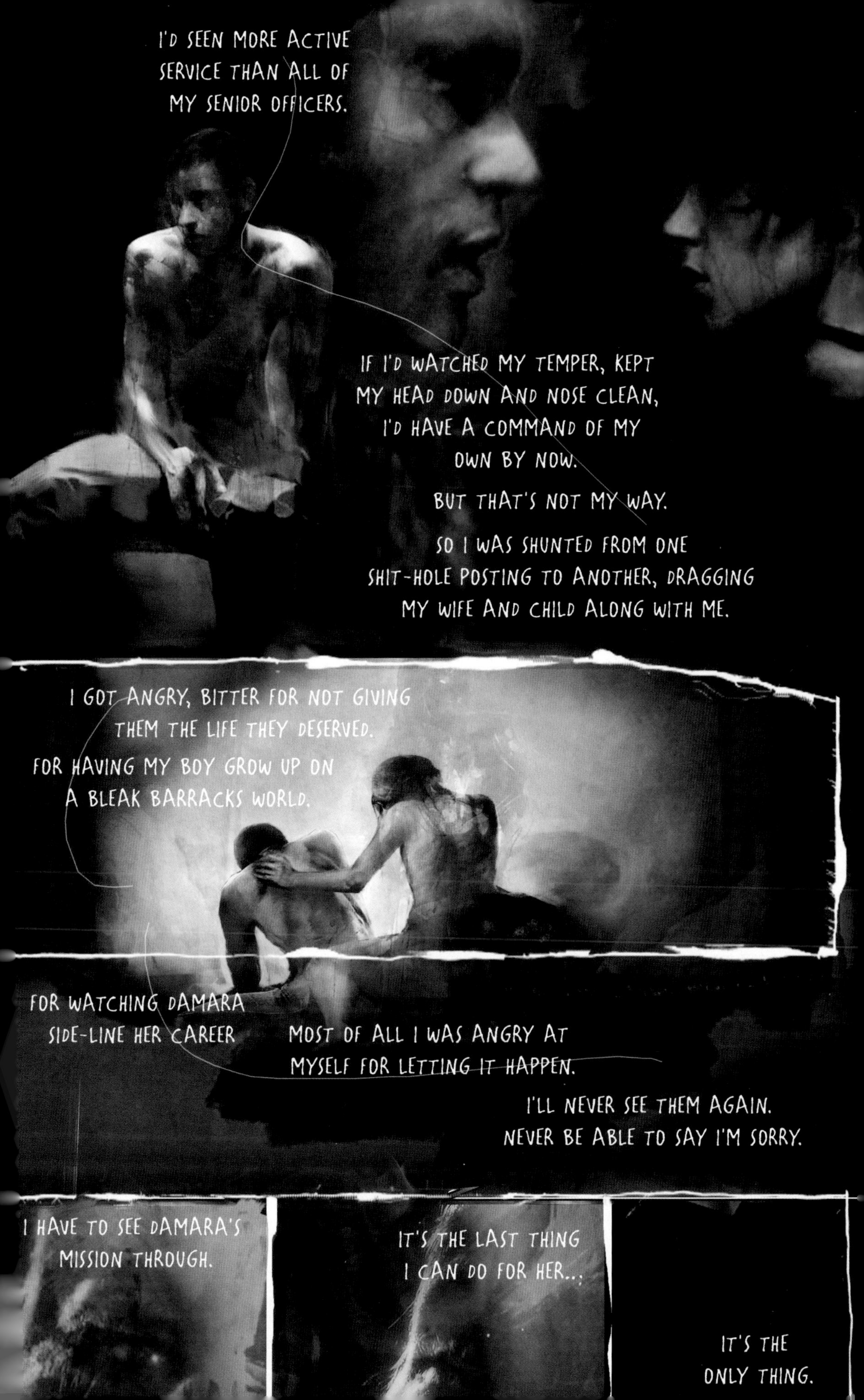
I'D SEEN MORE ACTIVE SERVICE THAN ALL OF MY SENIOR OFFICERS.
IF I'D WATCHED MY TEMPER, KEPT MY HEAD DOWN AND NOSE CLEAN, I'D HAVE A COMMAND OF MY OWN BY NOW.
BUT THAT'S NOT MY WAY.
SO I WAS SHUNTED FROM ONE SHIT-HOLE POSTING TO ANOTHER, DRAGGING MY WIFE AND CHILD ALONG WITH ME.
I GOT ANGRY, BITTER FOR NOT GIVING THEM THE LIFE THEY DESERVED.
FOR HAVING MY BOY GROW UP ON A BLEAK BARRACKS WORLD.
FOR WATCHING DAMARA SIDE-LINE HER CAREER
MOST OF ALL I WAS ANGRY AT MYSELF FOR LETTING IT HAPPEN.
I'LL NEVER SEE THEM AGAIN. NEVER BE ABLE TO SAY I'M SORRY.
I HAVE TO SEE DAMARA'S MISSION THROUGH.
IT'S THE LAST THING I CAN DO FOR HER...
IT'S THE ONLY THING.

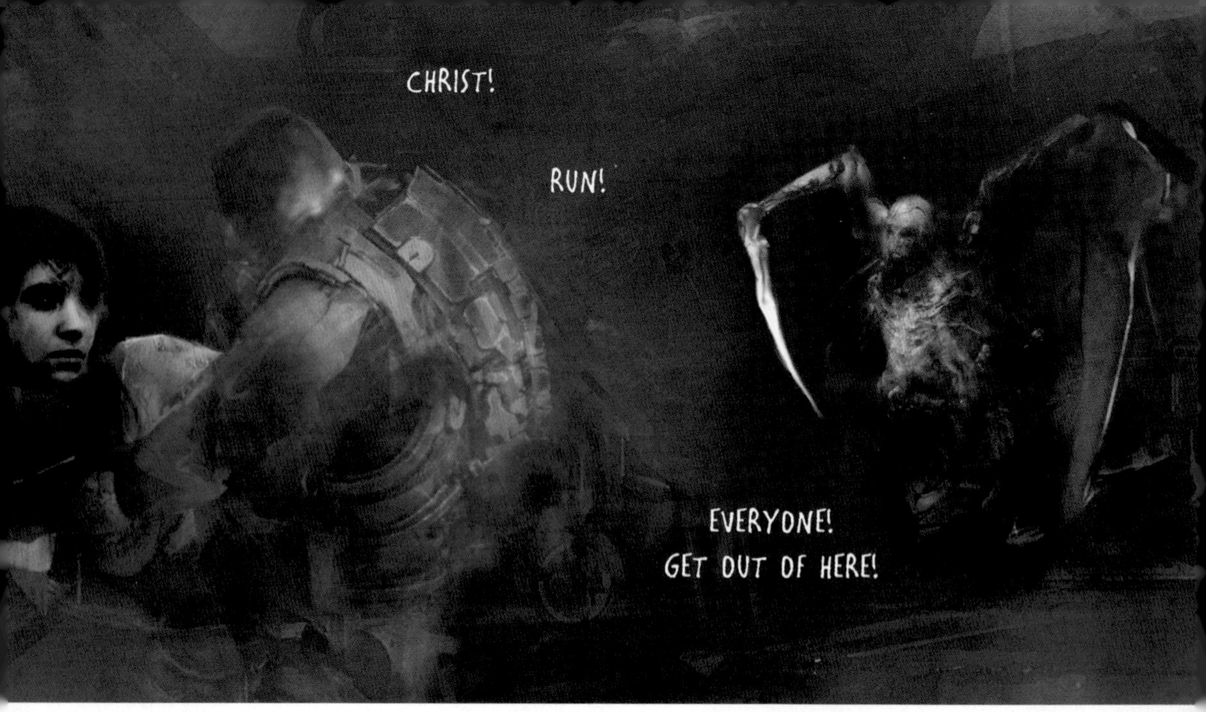
CHRIST!
RUN!
EVERYONE!
GET OUT OF HERE!

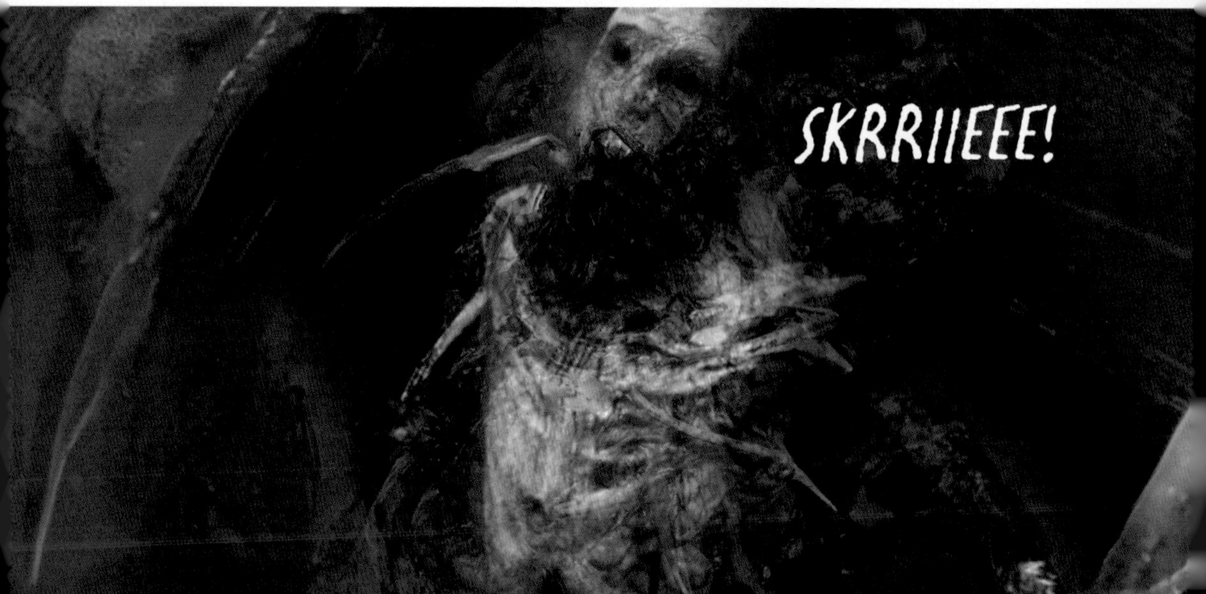
SKRRIIEEE!

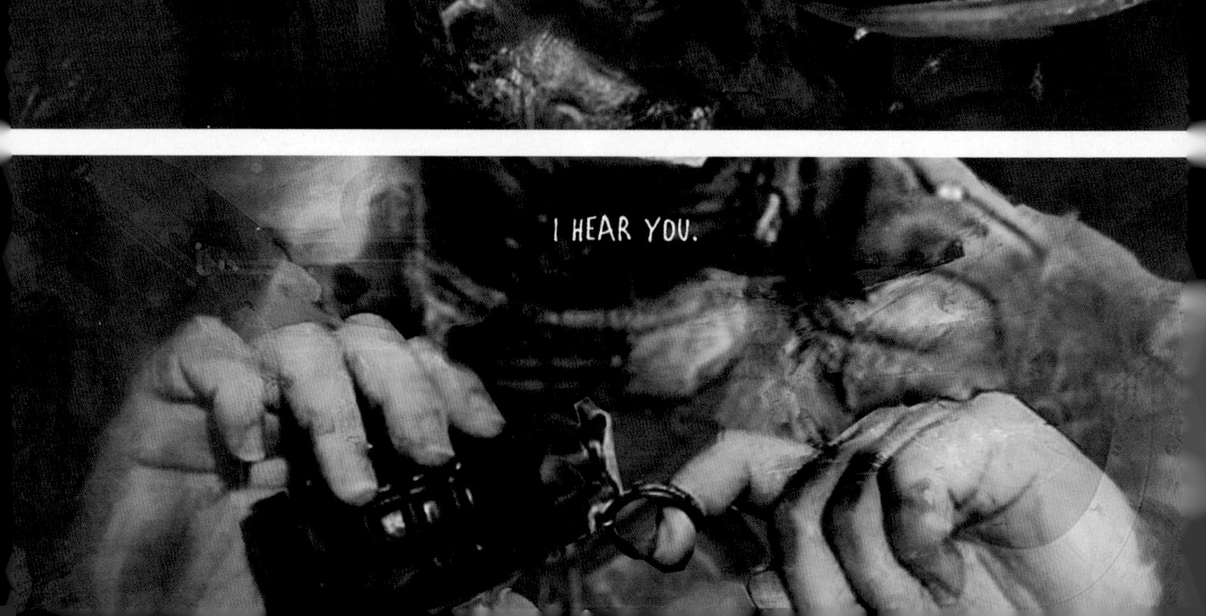
I HEAR YOU.

NEXT TIME, SIR. ORDERS OR NOT, WE DO IT MY WAY.

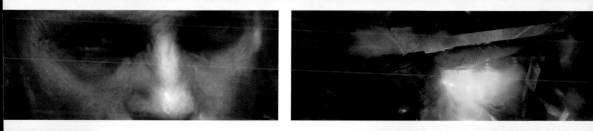

WELL...

AT LEAST IT CAN'T GET ANY WORSE.

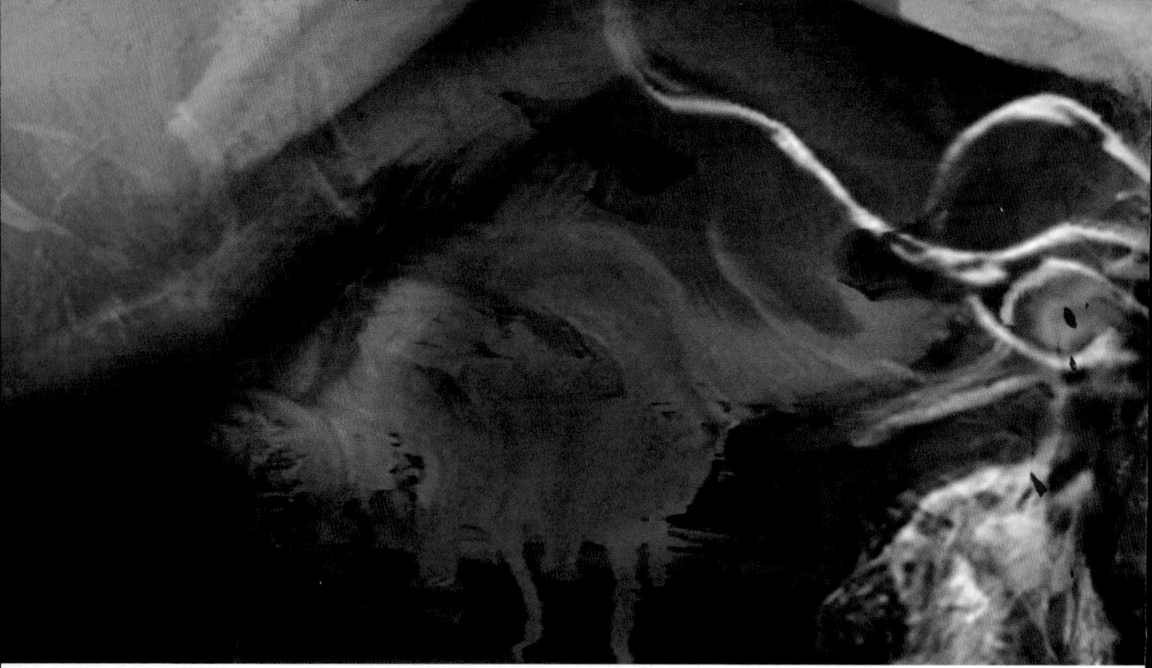

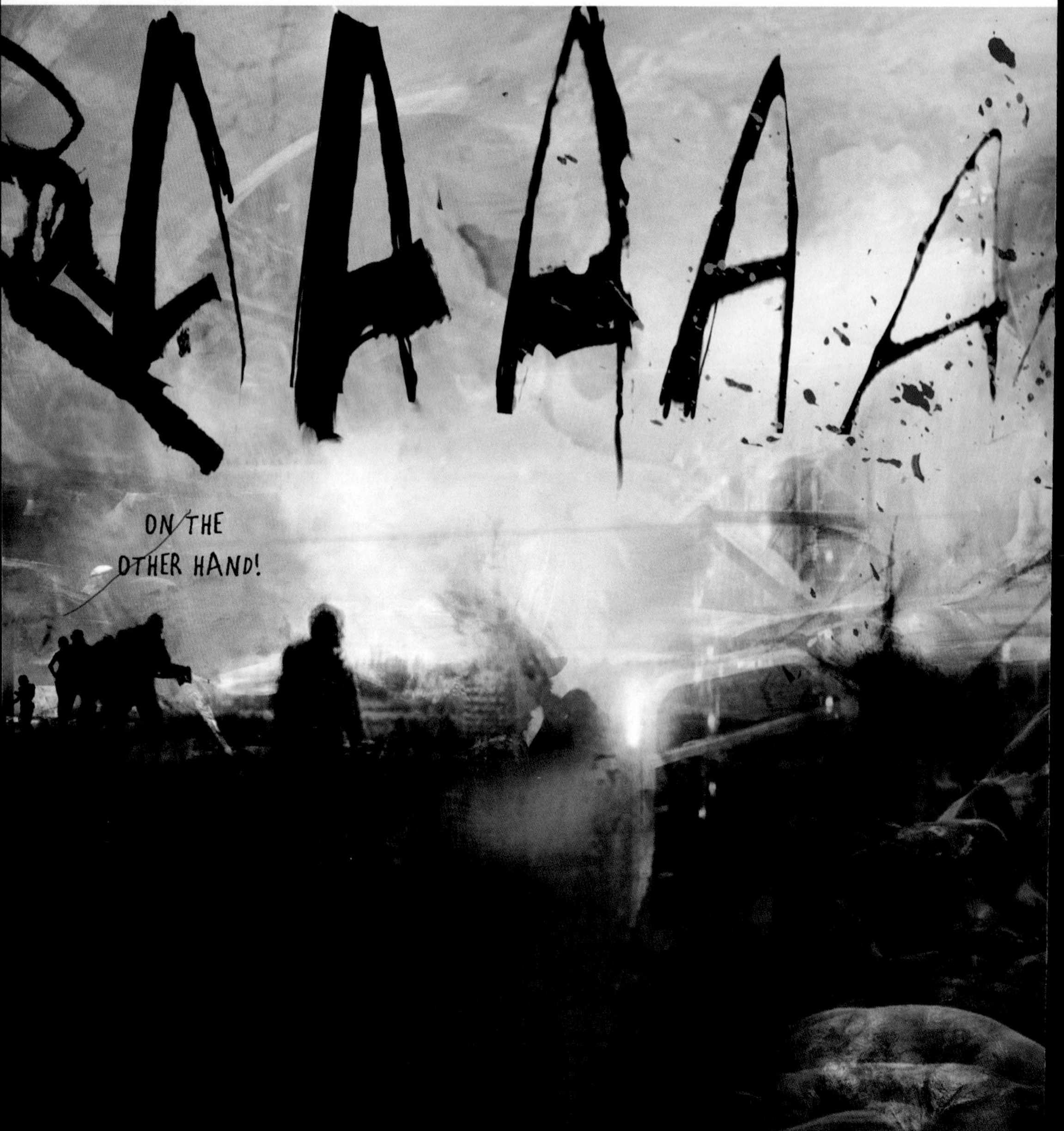
RAAAAA
ON THE OTHER HAND!

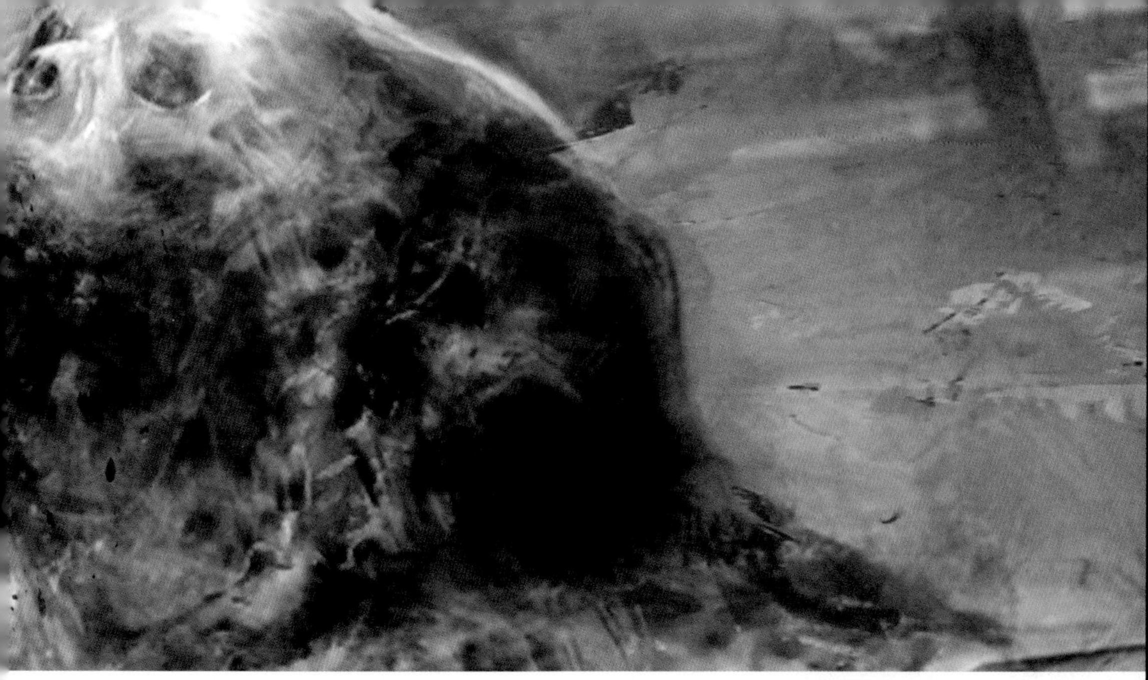

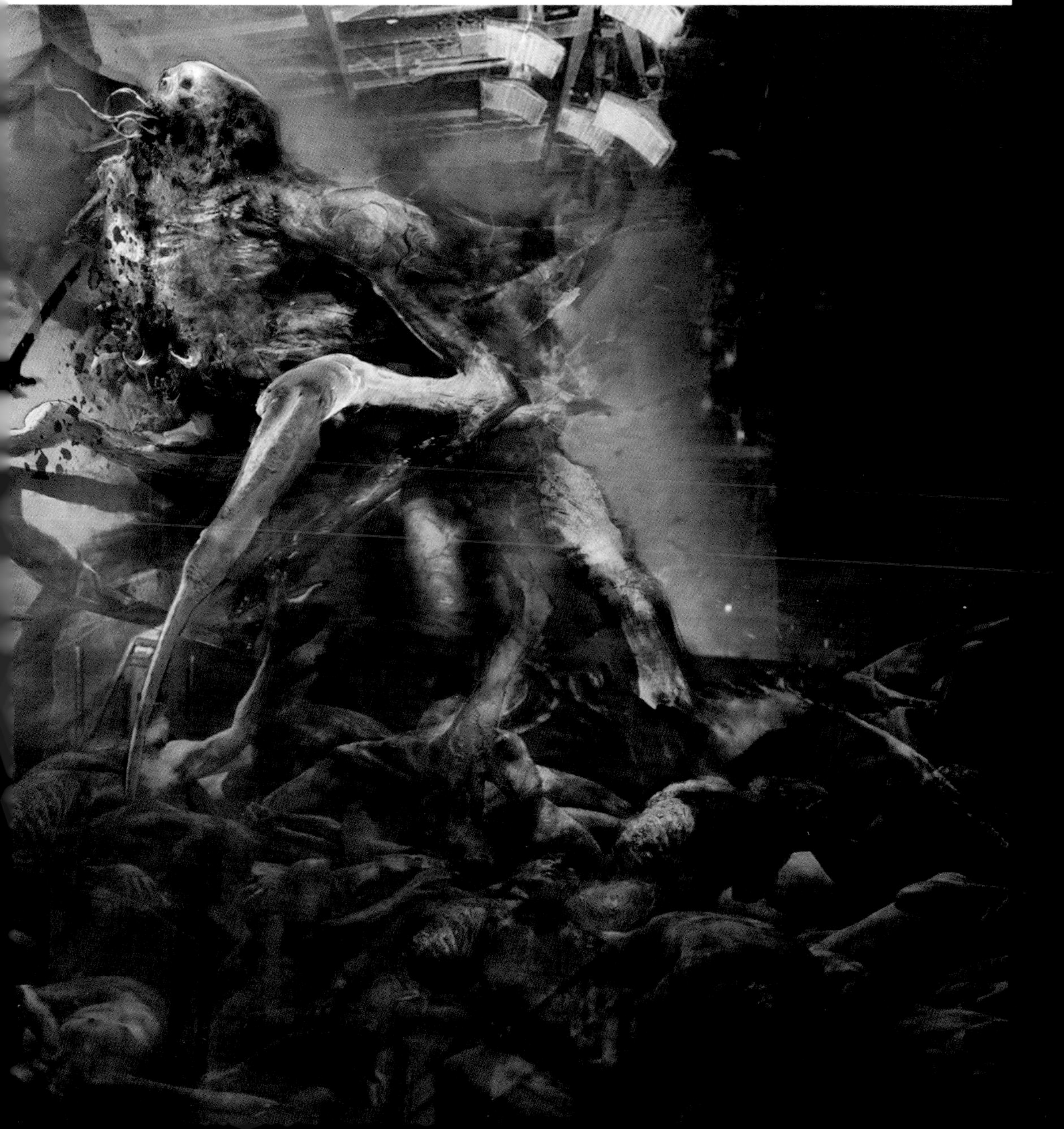

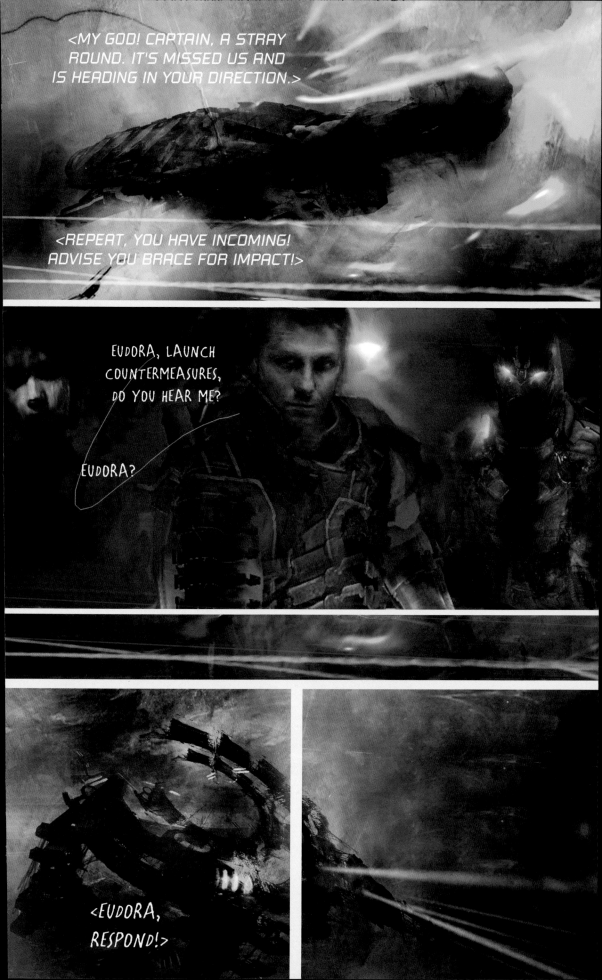

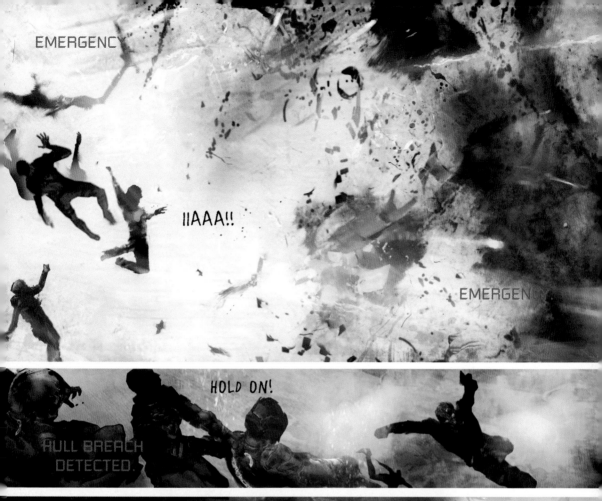

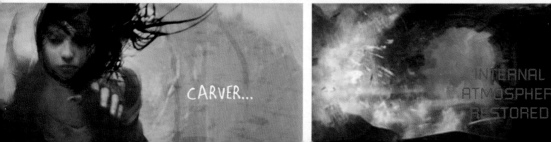

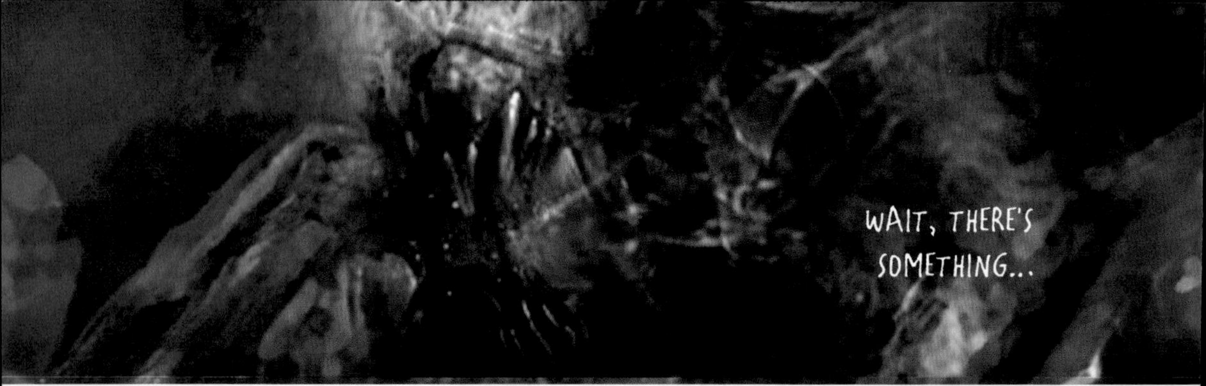
WAIT, THERE'S SOMETHING...

OH, NO!
MORE OF THEM!

THEY'VE BROKEN THROUGH!

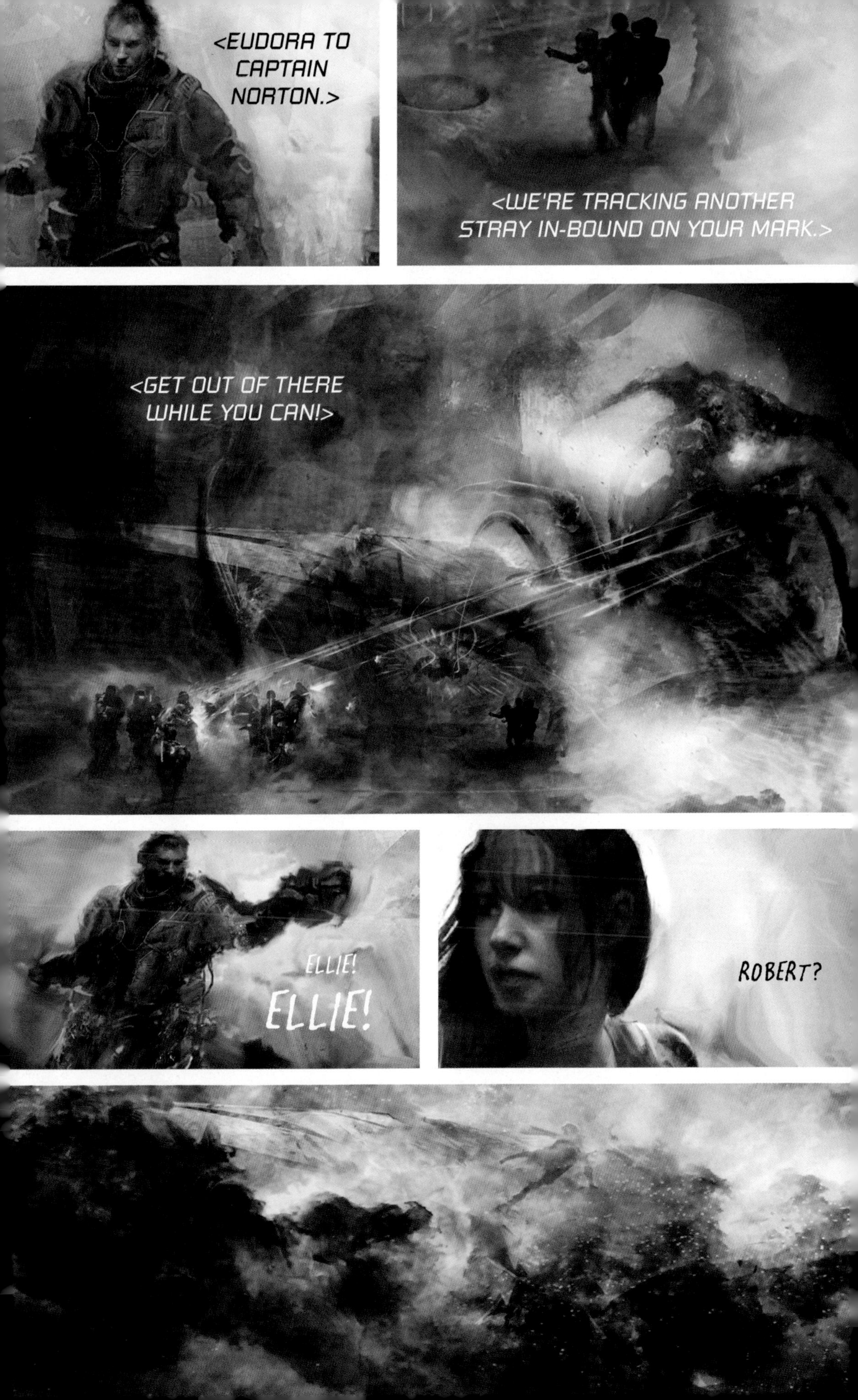
<EUDORA TO CAPTAIN NORTON.>
<WE'RE TRACKING ANOTHER STRAY IN-BOUND ON YOUR MARK.>
<GET OUT OF THERE WHILE YOU CAN!>
ELLIE!
ELLIE!
ROBERT?

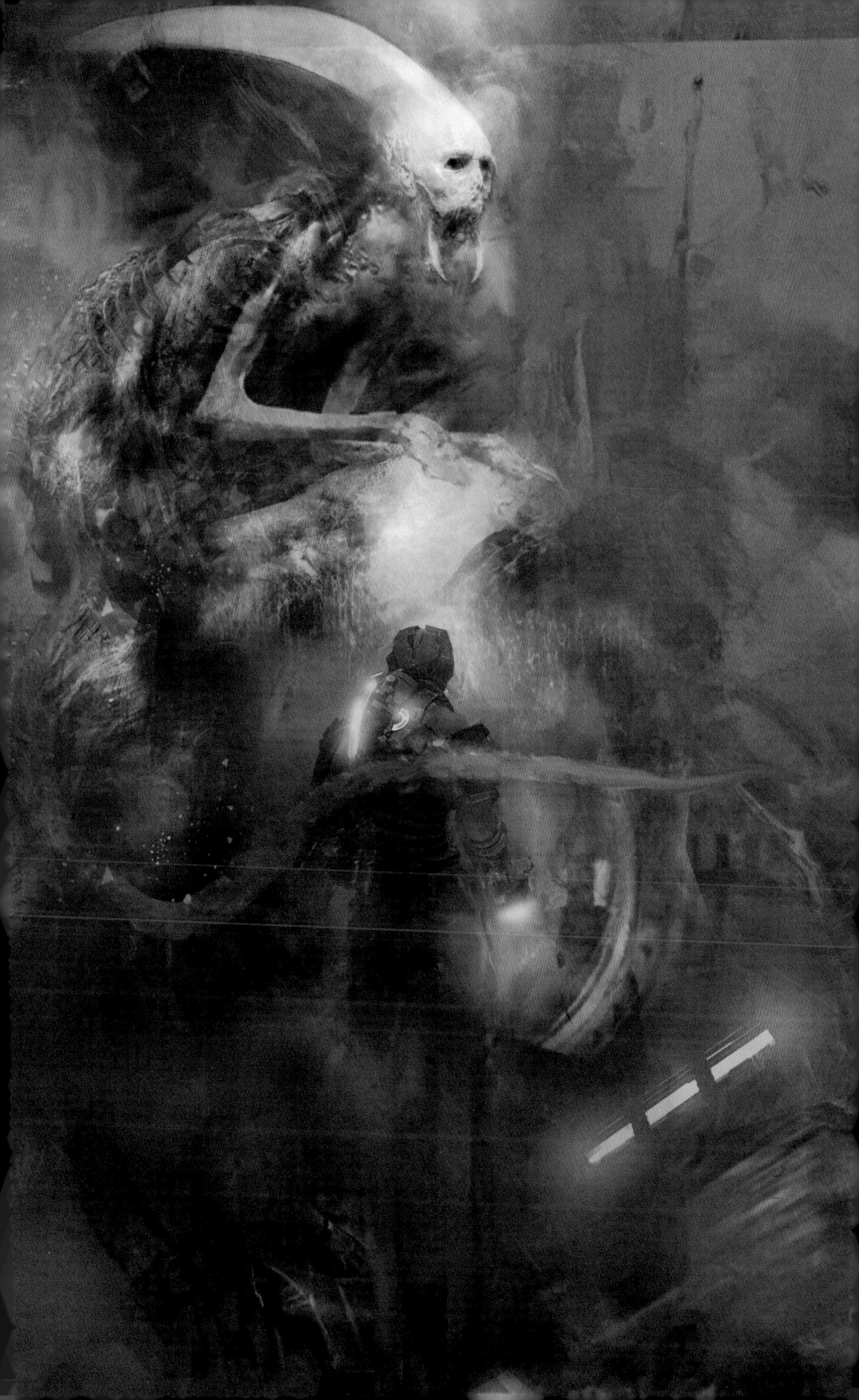

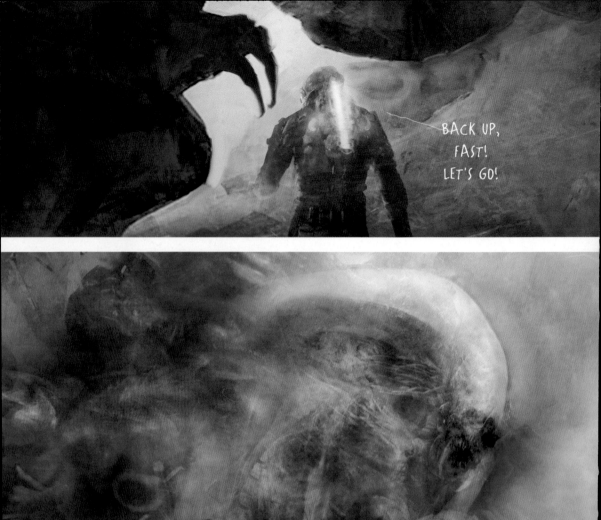

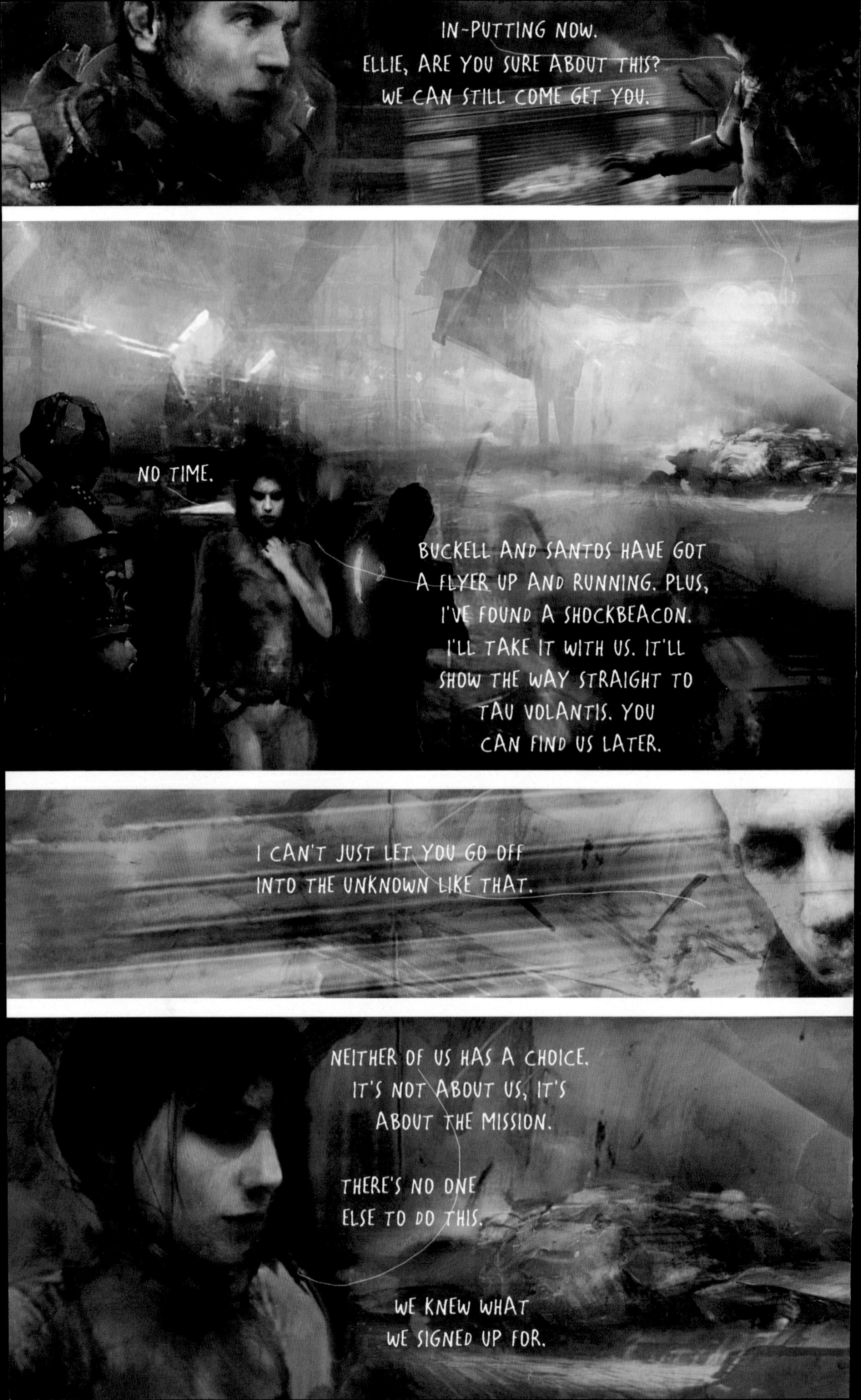
IN-PUTTING NOW.
ELLIE, ARE YOU SURE ABOUT THIS? WE CAN STILL COME GET YOU.
NO TIME.
BUCKELL AND SANTOS HAVE GOT A FLYER UP AND RUNNING. PLUS, I'VE FOUND A SHOCKBEACON. I'LL TAKE IT WITH US. IT'LL SHOW THE WAY STRAIGHT TO TAU VOLANTIS. YOU CAN FIND US LATER.
I CAN'T JUST LET YOU GO OFF INTO THE UNKNOWN LIKE THAT.
NEITHER OF US HAS A CHOICE. IT'S NOT ABOUT US, IT'S ABOUT THE MISSION.
THERE'S NO ONE ELSE TO DO THIS.
WE KNEW WHAT WE SIGNED UP FOR.

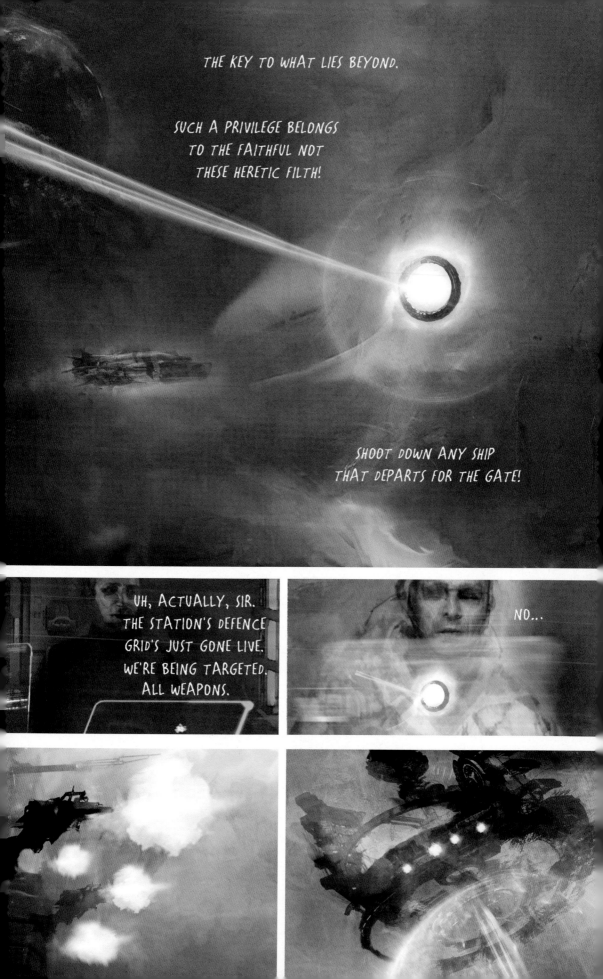

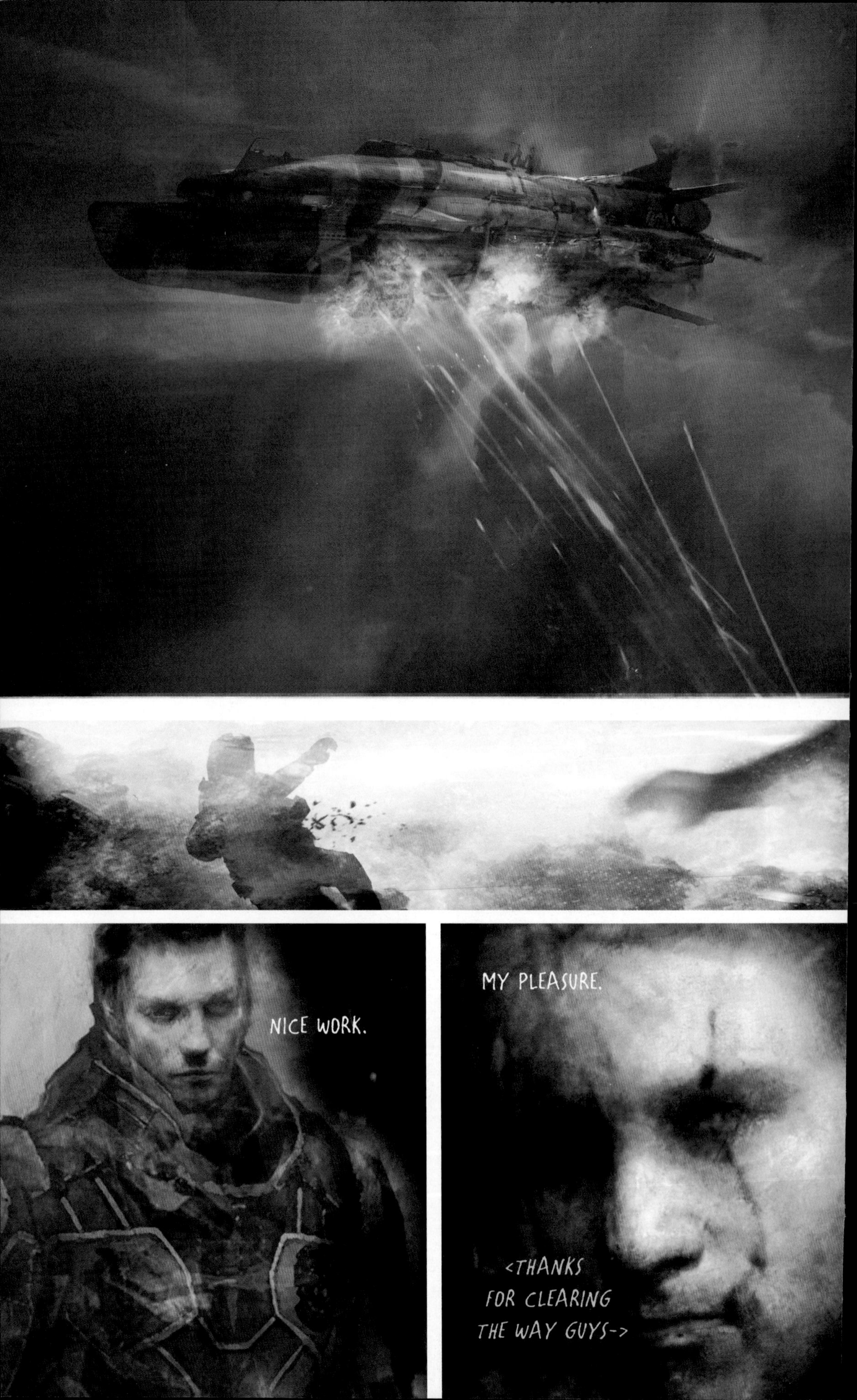
NICE WORK.
MY PLEASURE.
<THANKS FOR CLEARING THE WAY GUYS->

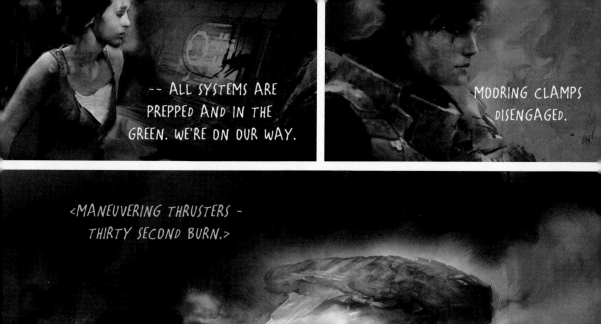

-- ALL SYSTEMS ARE PREPPED AND IN THE GREEN. WE'RE ON OUR WAY.

MOORING CLAMPS DISENGAGED.

<MANEUVERING THRUSTERS - THIRTY SECOND BURN.>

<COURSE LAID IN FOR SHOCK GATE THRESHOLD.>

ELLIE...
GOOD LUCK HONEY.
I LOVE YOU.

I LOVE YOU TOO.
COME GET ME
SOON, OK?

YOU CAN
COUNT ON IT.

ACTIVATE YOUR MAGNETIC GRAPPLES!

CARVER, YOU OK?
YEAH. JUST TRYING TO HOLD ONTO MY LUNCH.
I FORGOT WHY I HATED ZERO-G COMBAT TRAINING SO MUCH.

NORTON TO EUDORA, WE'RE OUT!

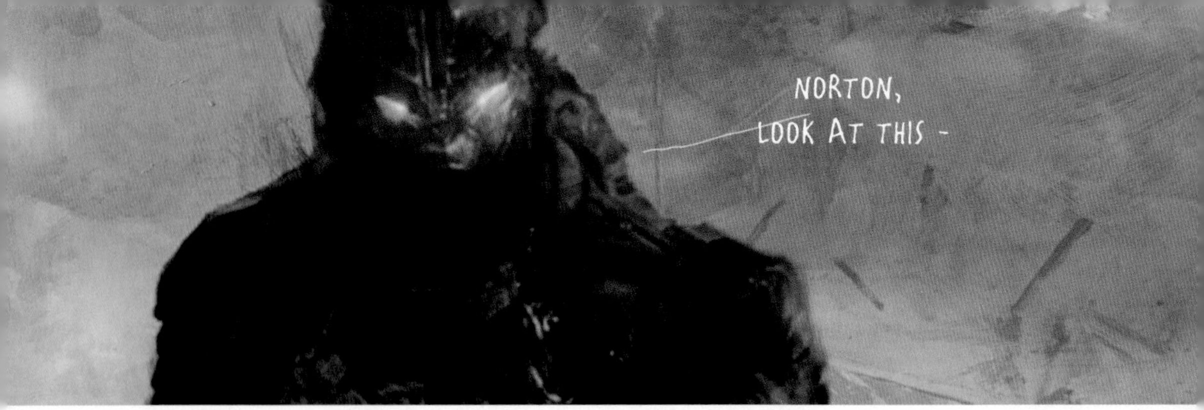
NORTON, LOOK AT THIS -

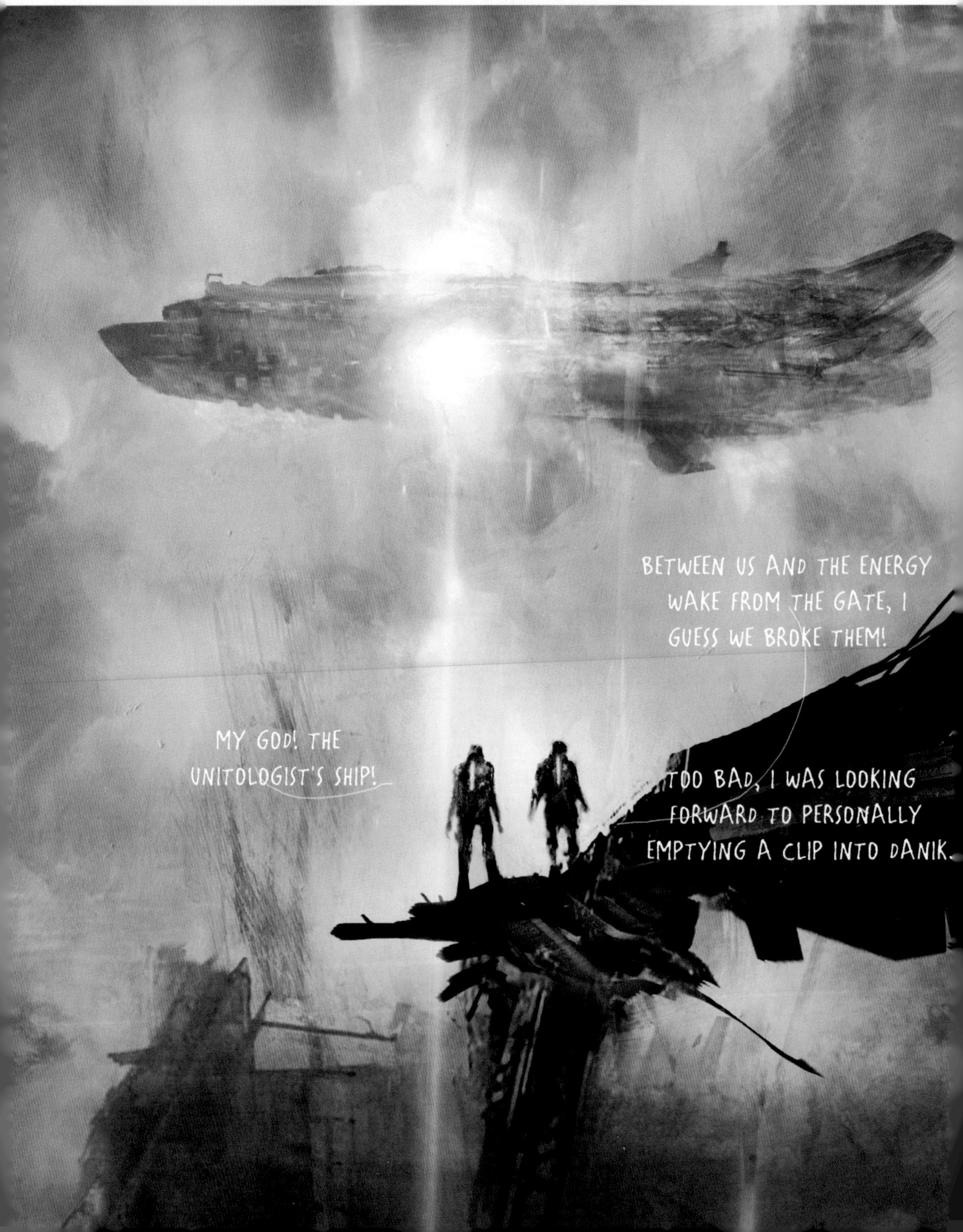
MY GOD! THE UNITOLOGIST'S SHIP!
BETWEEN US AND THE ENERGY WAKE FROM THE GATE, I GUESS WE BROKE THEM!
TOO BAD, I WAS LOOKING FORWARD TO PERSONALLY EMPTYING A CLIP INTO DANIK.

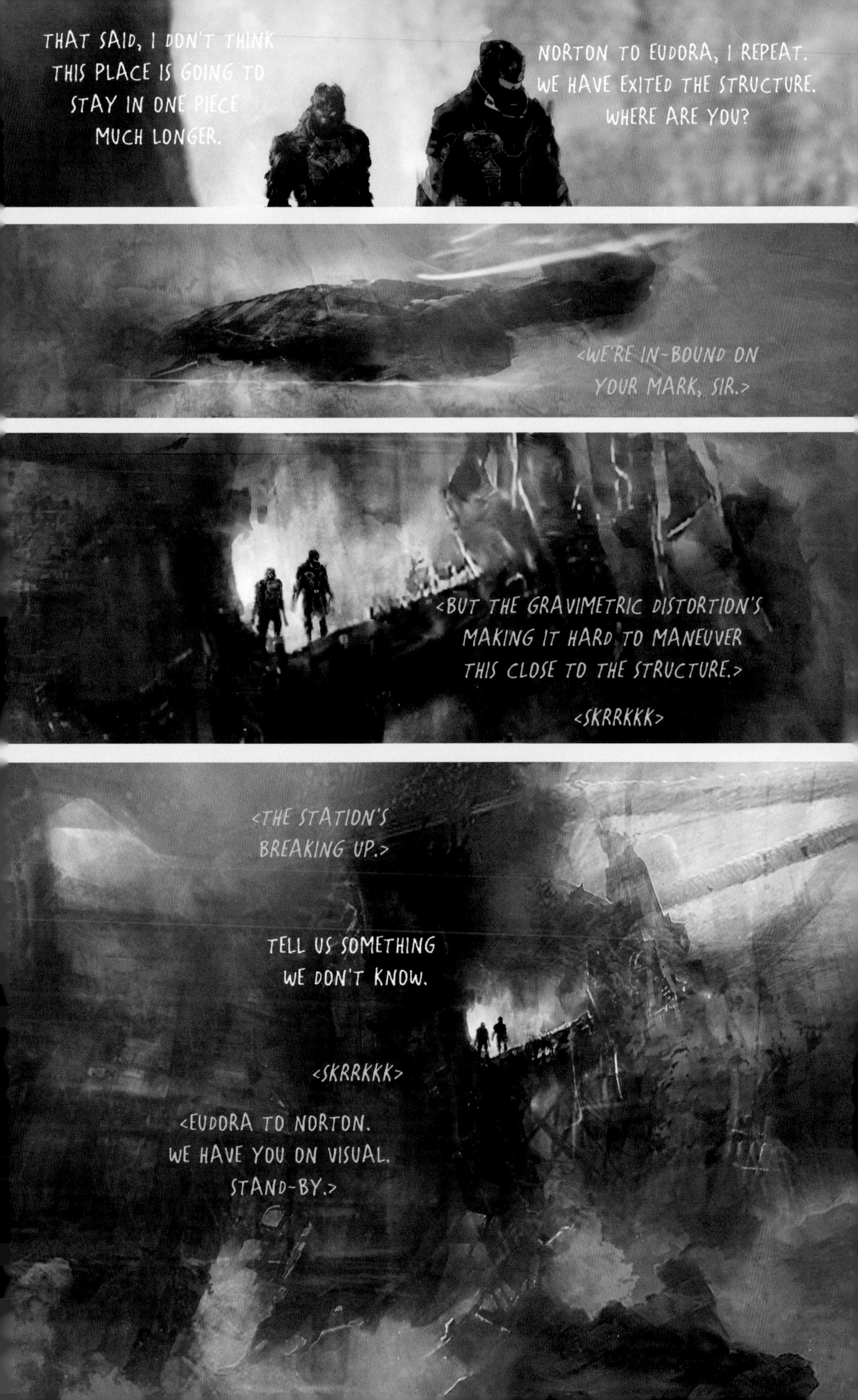
THAT SAID, I DON'T THINK THIS PLACE IS GOING TO STAY IN ONE PIECE MUCH LONGER.
NORTON TO EUDORA, I REPEAT. WE HAVE EXITED THE STRUCTURE. WHERE ARE YOU?
<WE'RE IN-BOUND ON YOUR MARK, SIR.>
<BUT THE GRAVIMETRIC DISTORTION'S MAKING IT HARD TO MANEUVER THIS CLOSE TO THE STRUCTURE.>
<SKRRKKK>
<THE STATION'S BREAKING UP.>
TELL US SOMETHING WE DON'T KNOW.
<SKRRKKK>
<EUDORA TO NORTON. WE HAVE YOU ON VISUAL. STAND-BY.>

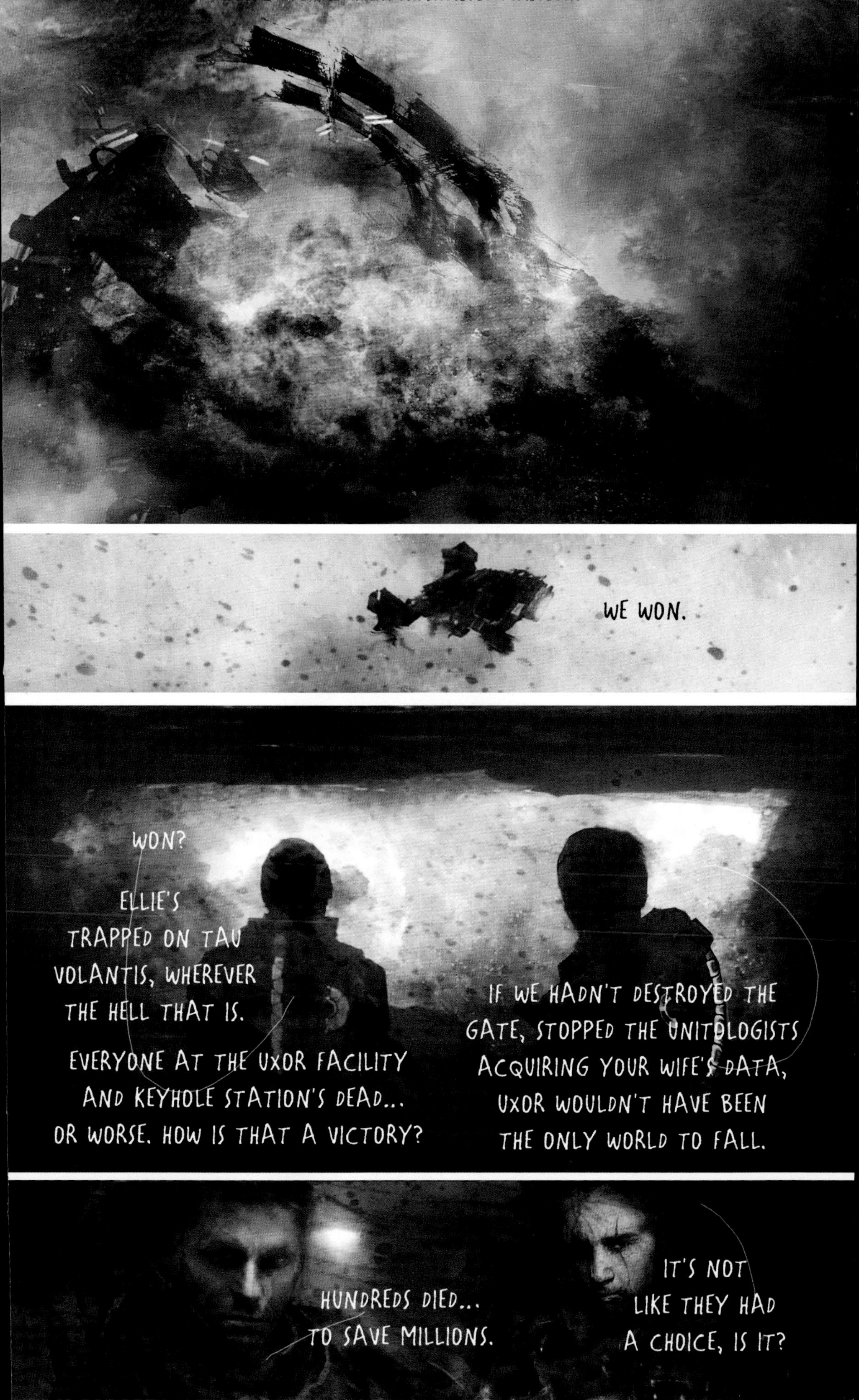
WE WON.
WON?
ELLIE'S TRAPPED ON TAU VOLANTIS, WHEREVER THE HELL THAT IS.
EVERYONE AT THE UXOR FACILITY AND KEYHOLE STATION'S DEAD... OR WORSE. HOW IS THAT A VICTORY?
IF WE HADN'T DESTROYED THE GATE, STOPPED THE UNITOLOGISTS ACQUIRING YOUR WIFE'S DATA, UXOR WOULDN'T HAVE BEEN THE ONLY WORLD TO FALL.
HUNDREDS DIED... TO SAVE MILLIONS.
IT'S NOT LIKE THEY HAD A CHOICE, IS IT?

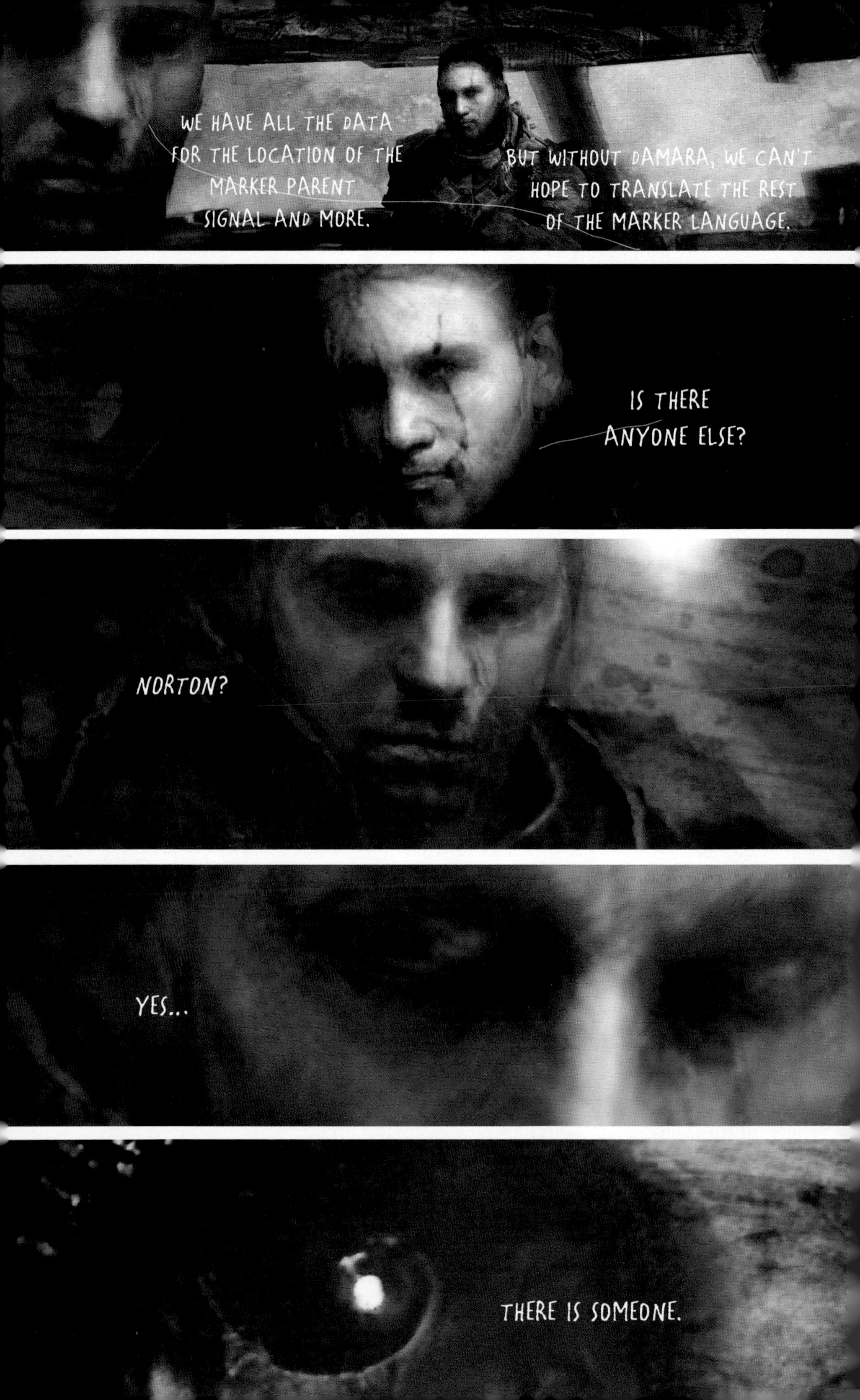
WE HAVE ALL THE DATA FOR THE LOCATION OF THE MARKER PARENT SIGNAL AND MORE.
BUT WITHOUT DAMARA, WE CAN'T HOPE TO TRANSLATE THE REST OF THE MARKER LANGUAGE.
IS THERE ANYONE ELSE?
NORTON?
YES...
THERE IS SOMEONE.

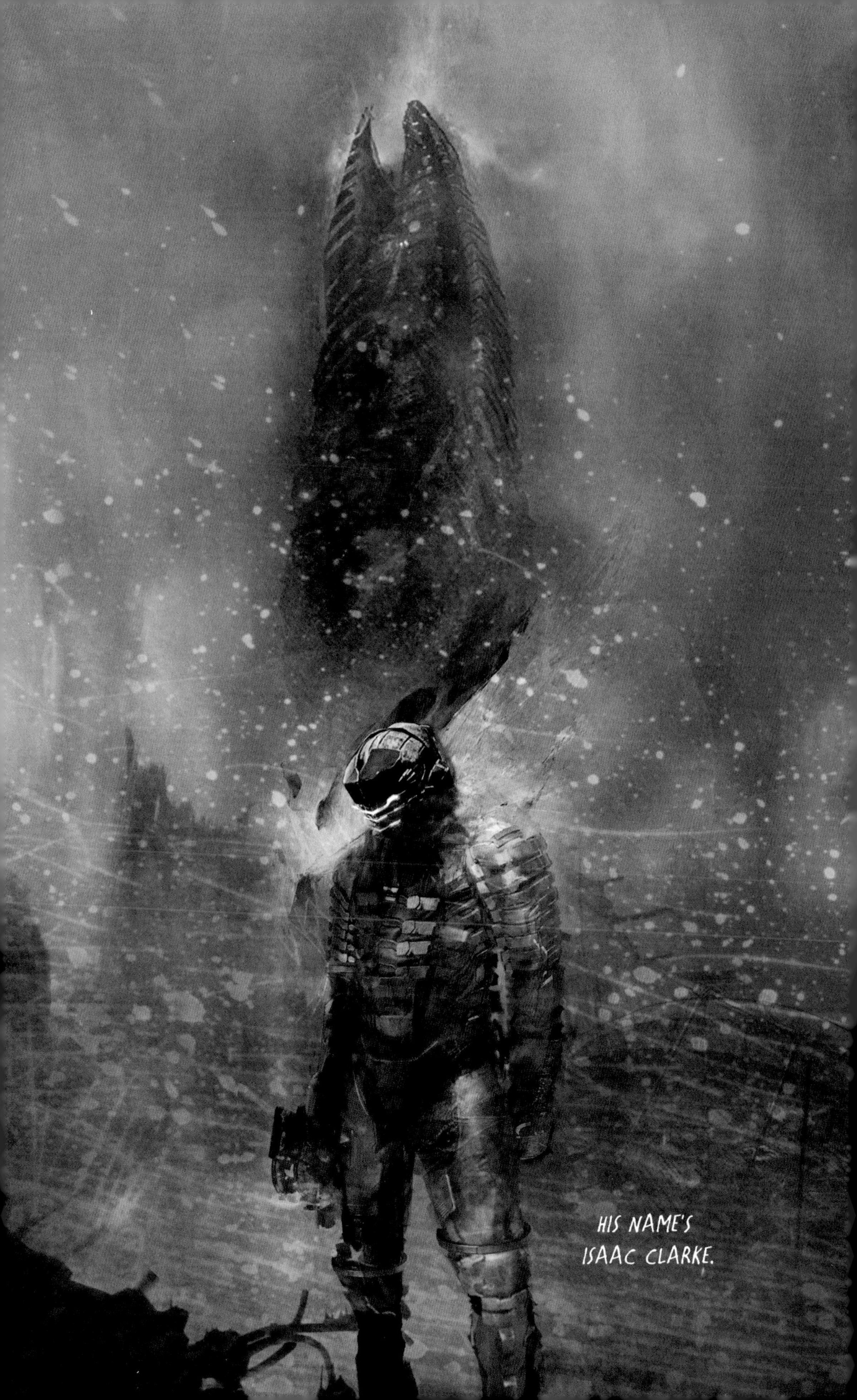
HIS NAME'S
ISAAC CLARKE.

DEAD SPACE
LIBERATION
GALLERY

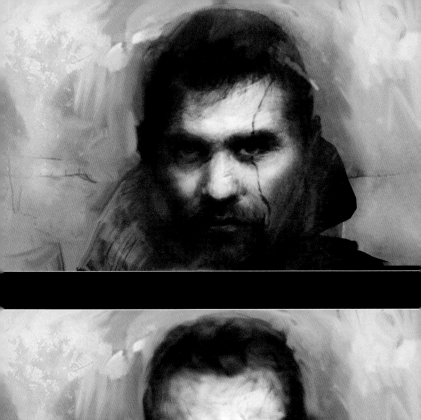

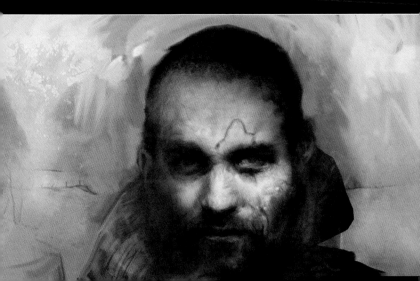

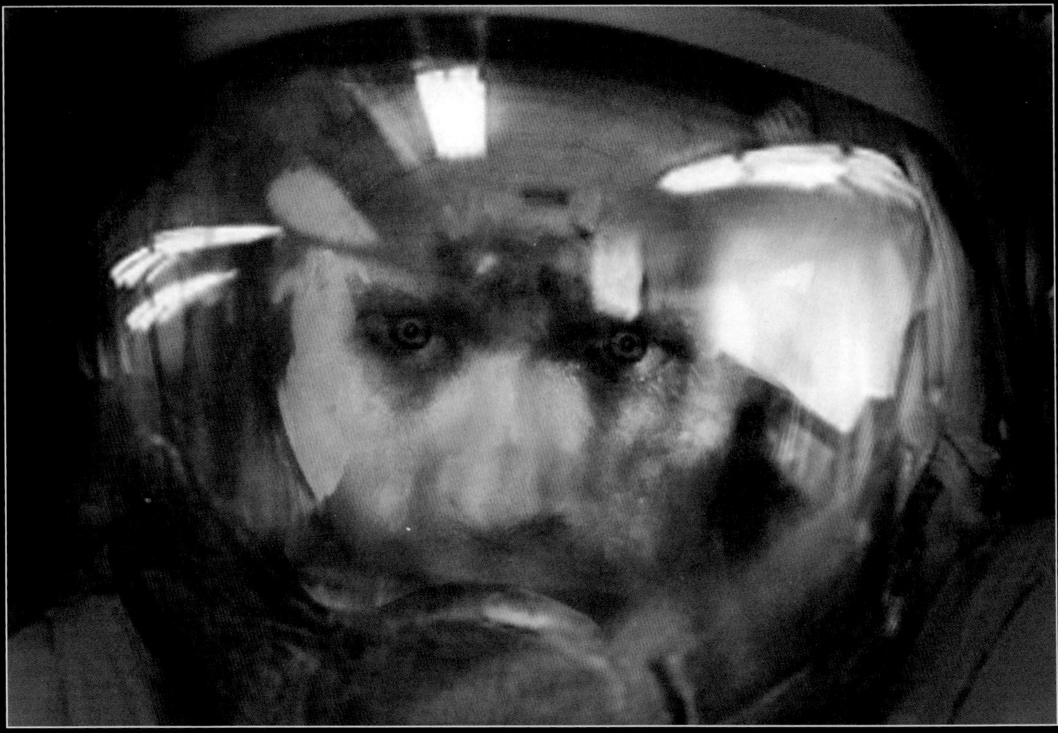

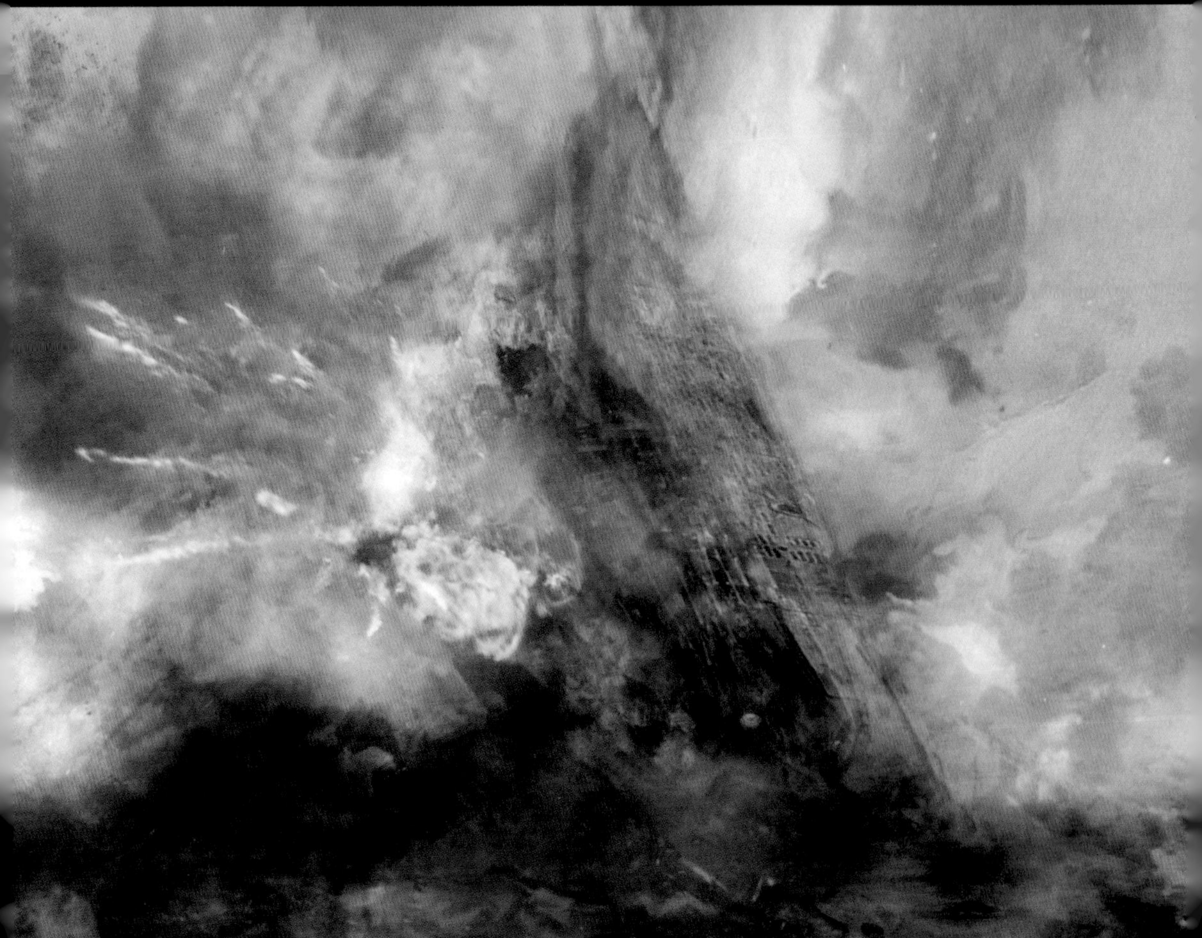

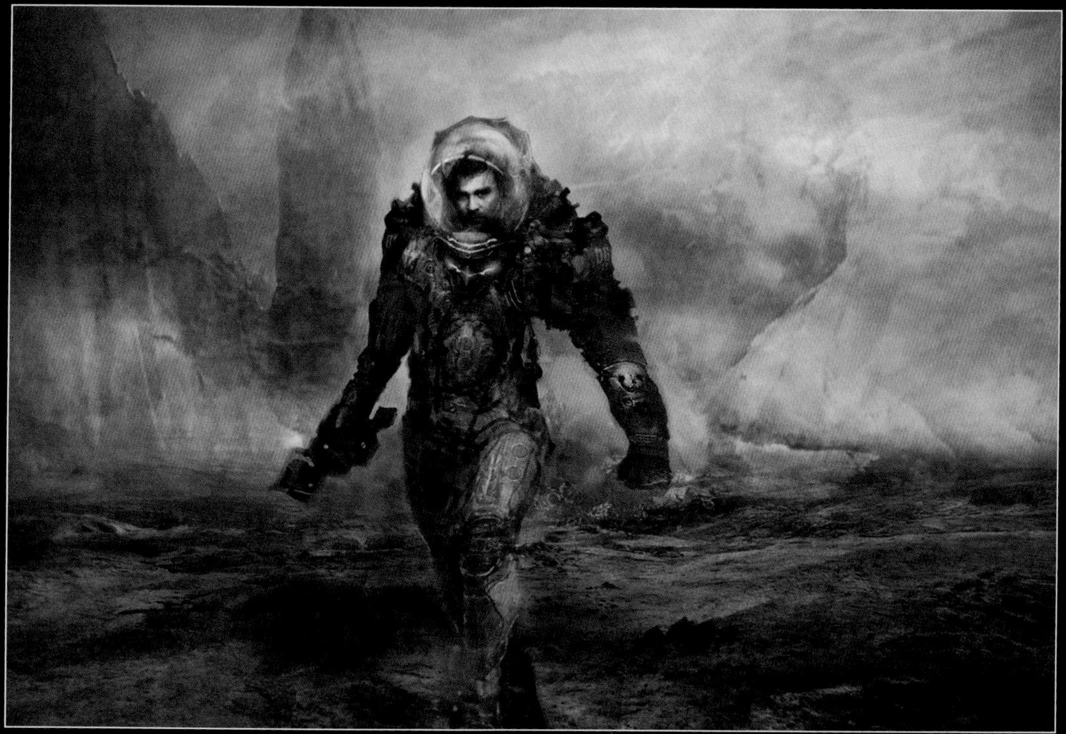

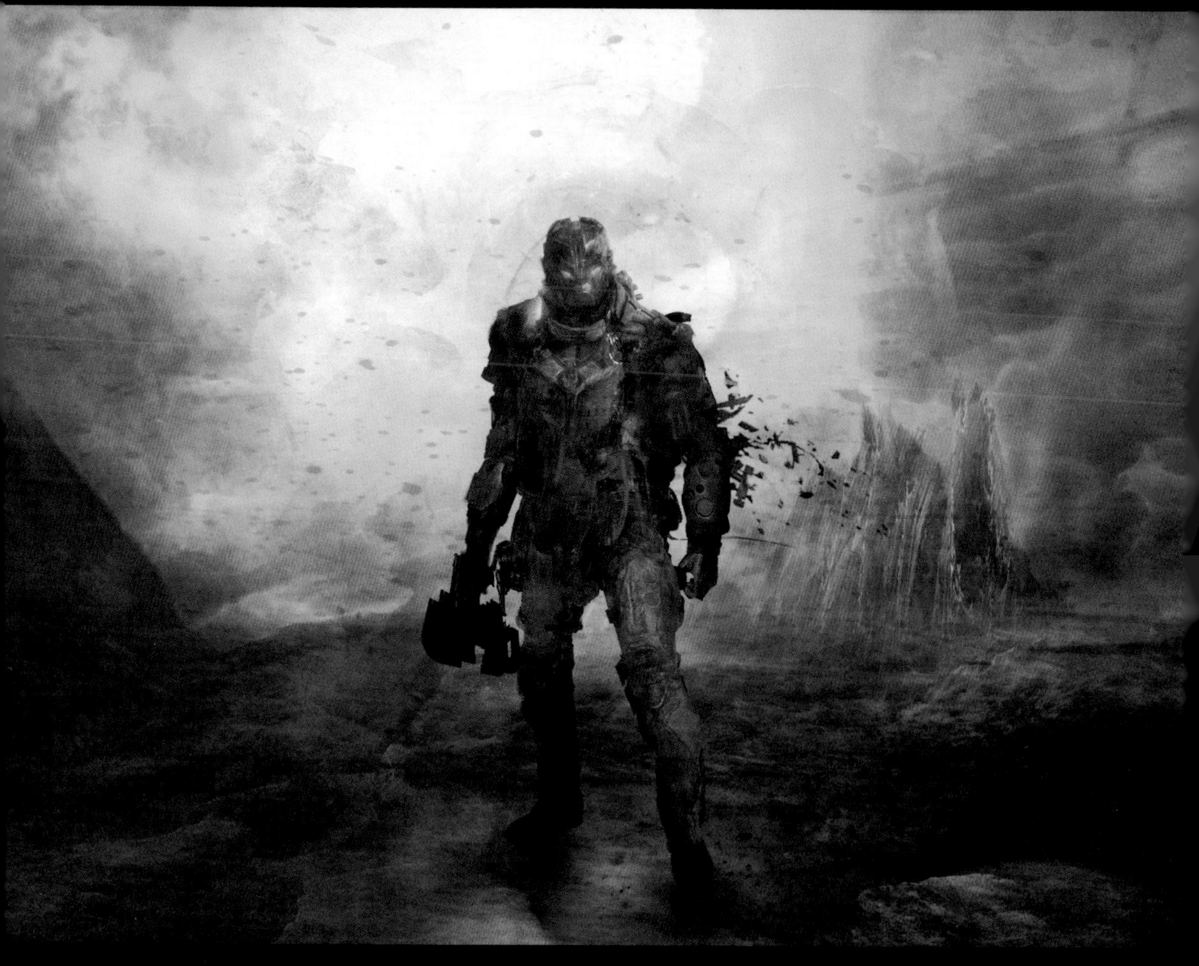

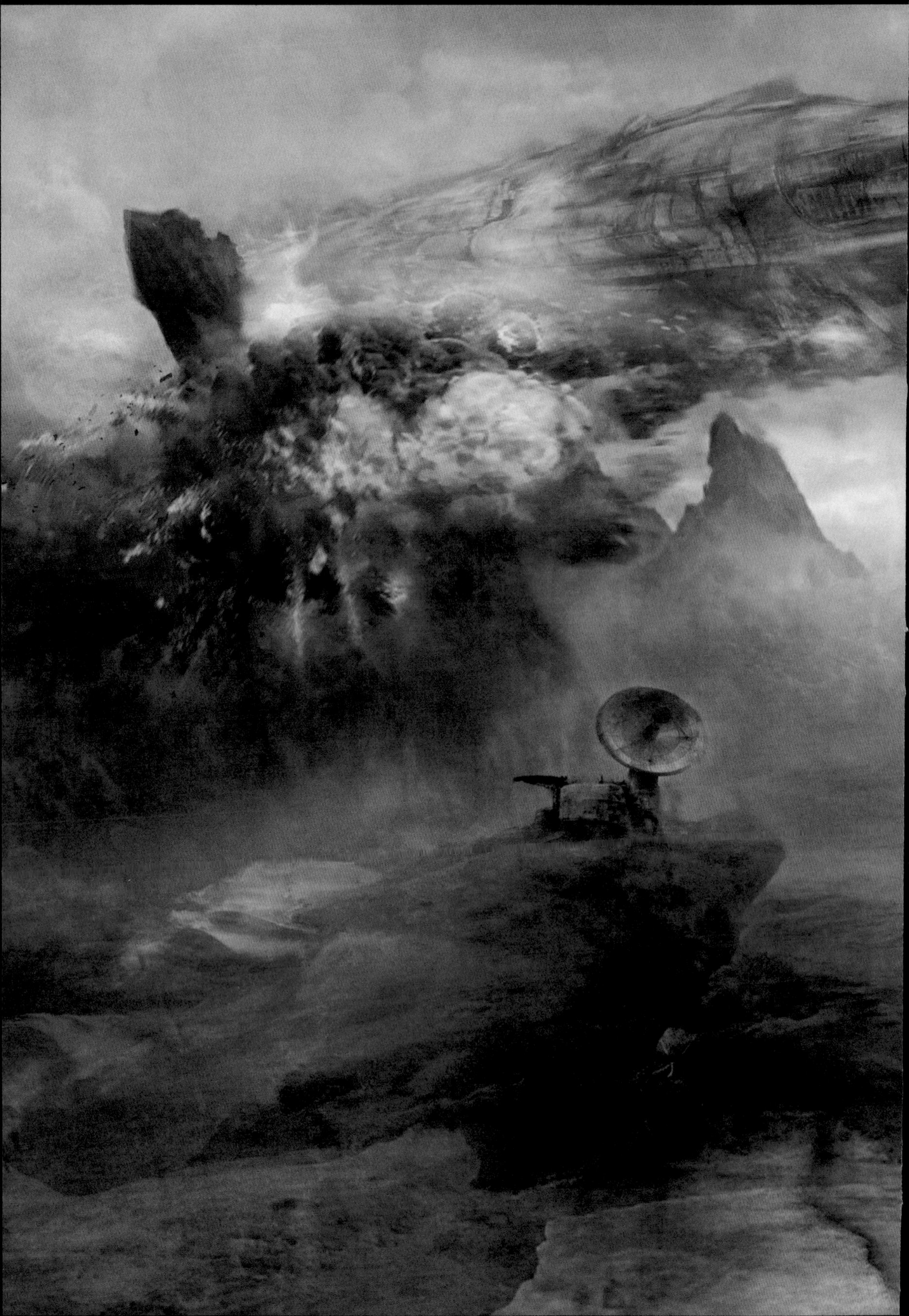

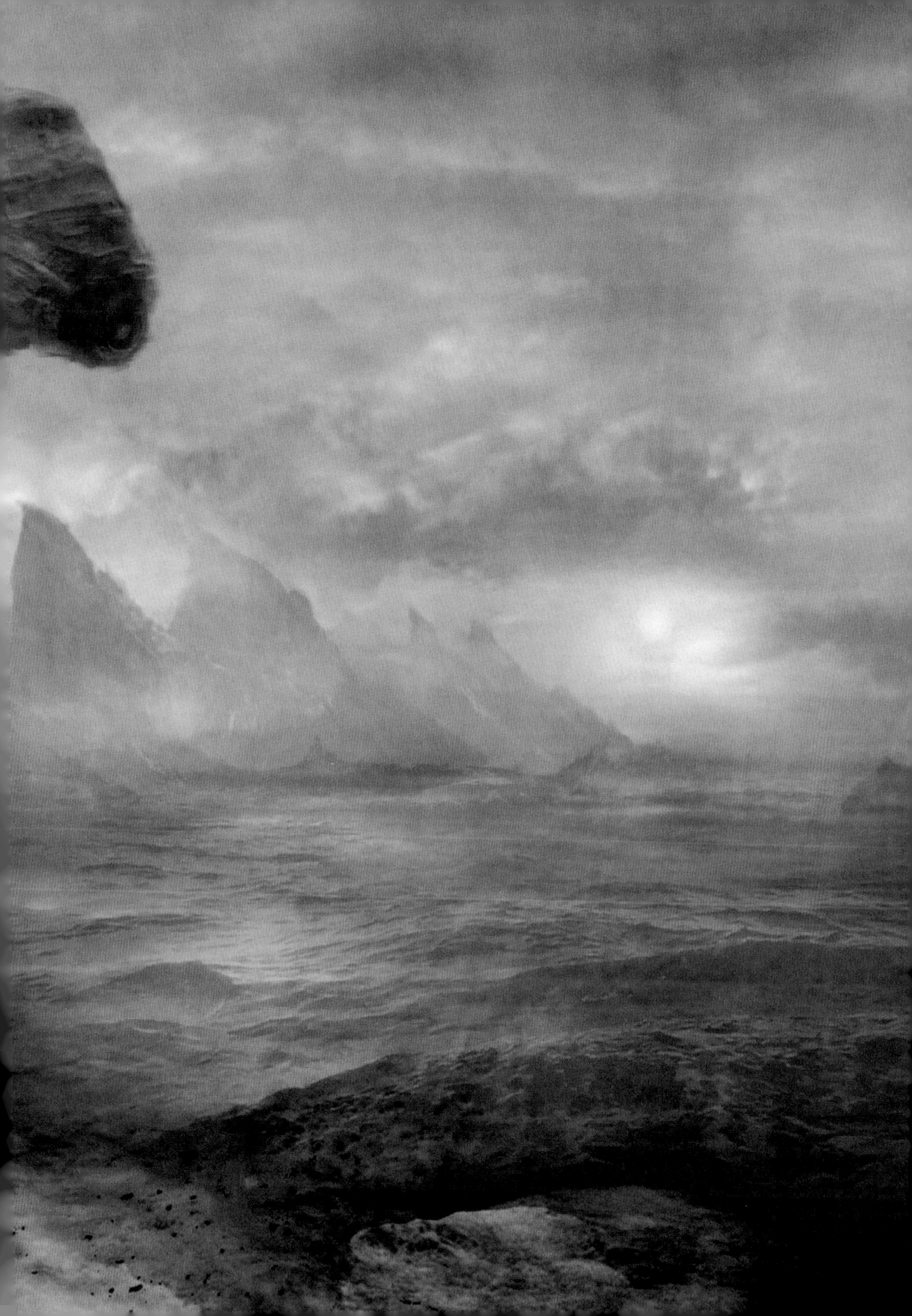

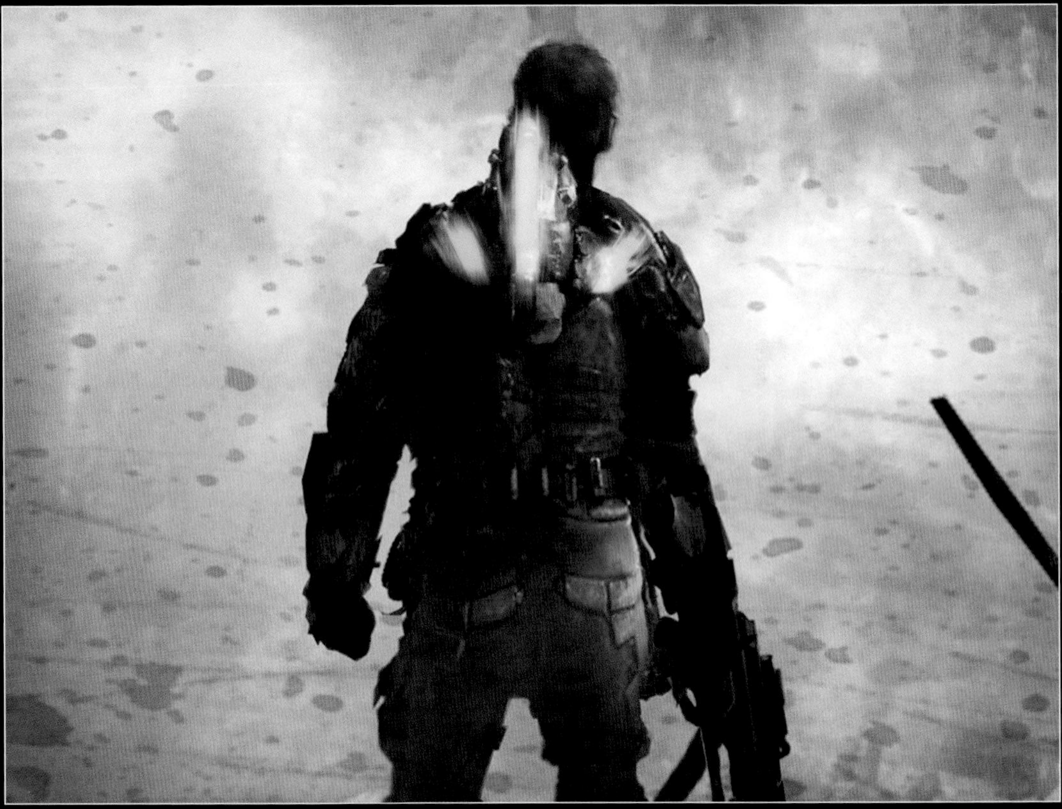

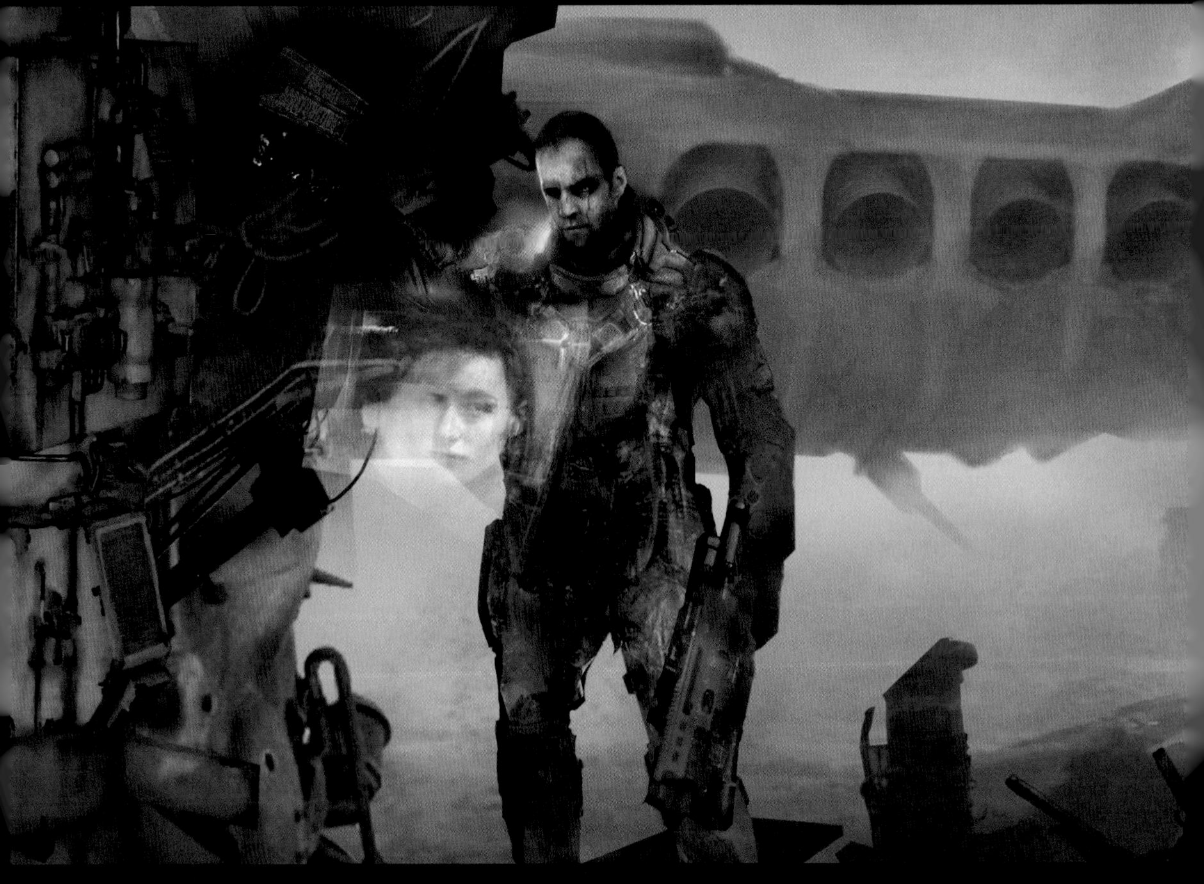

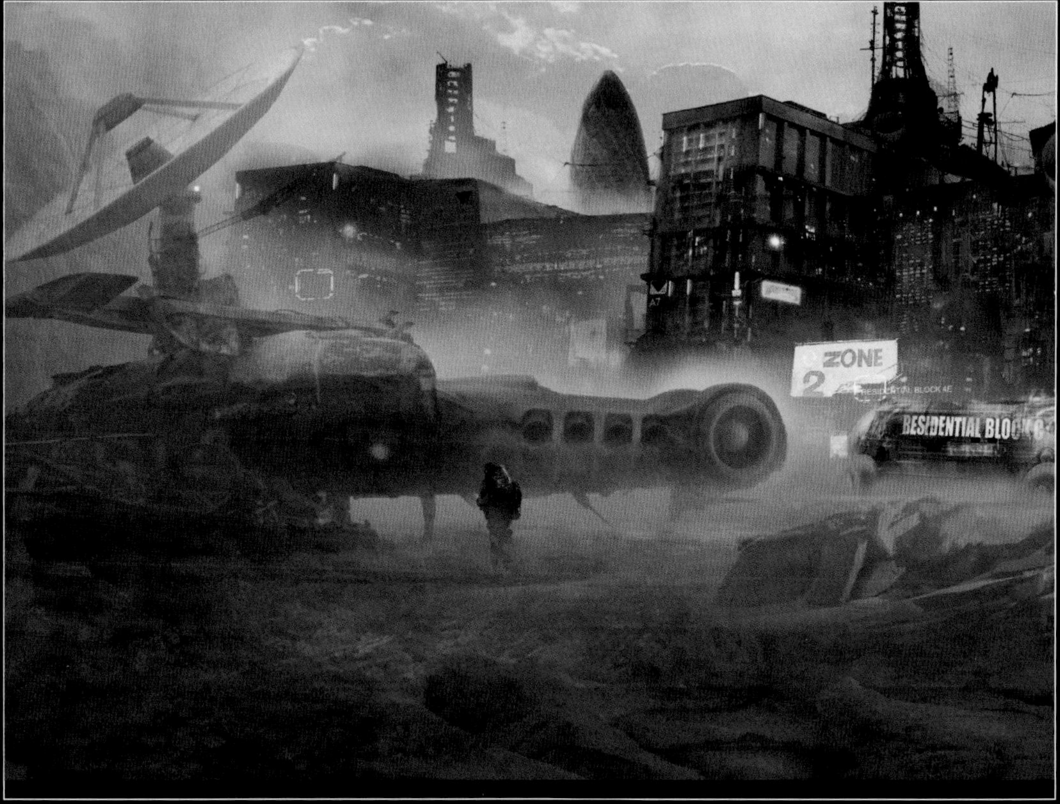
ZONE
2
RESIDENTIAL

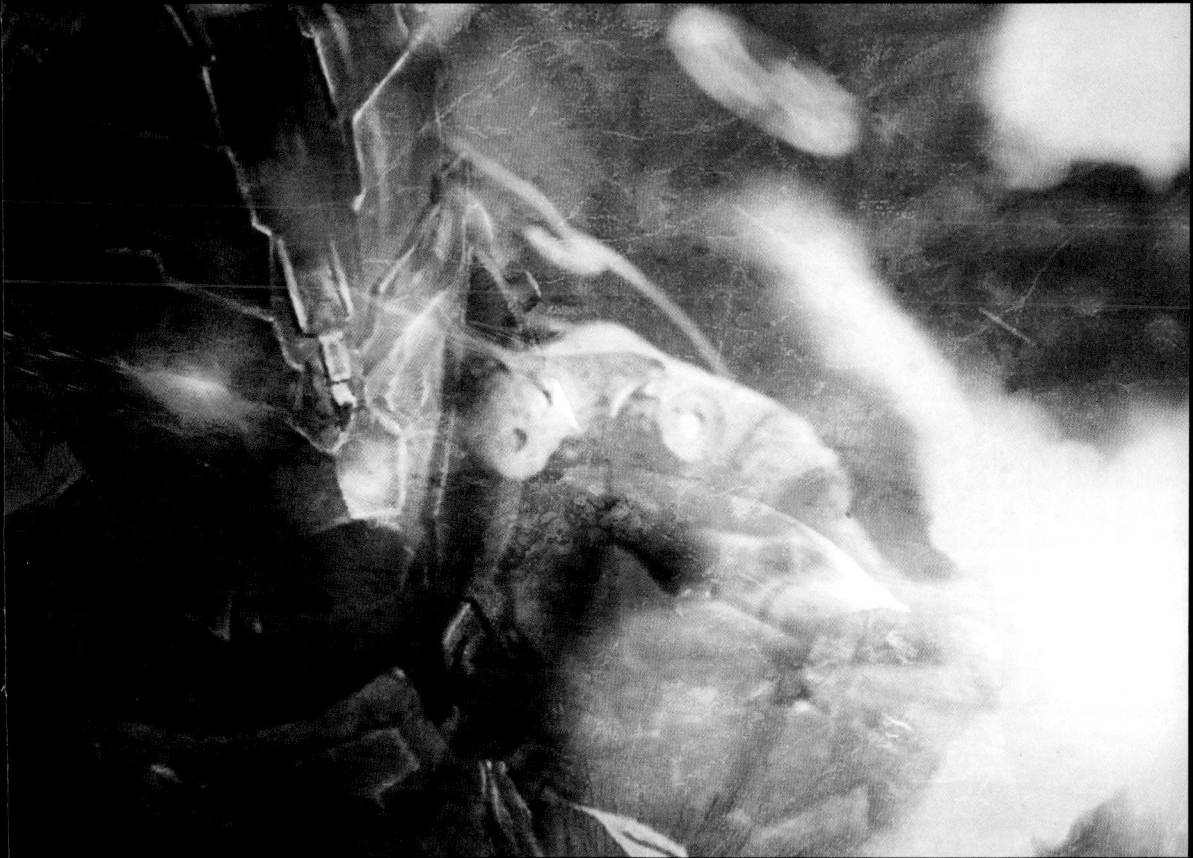

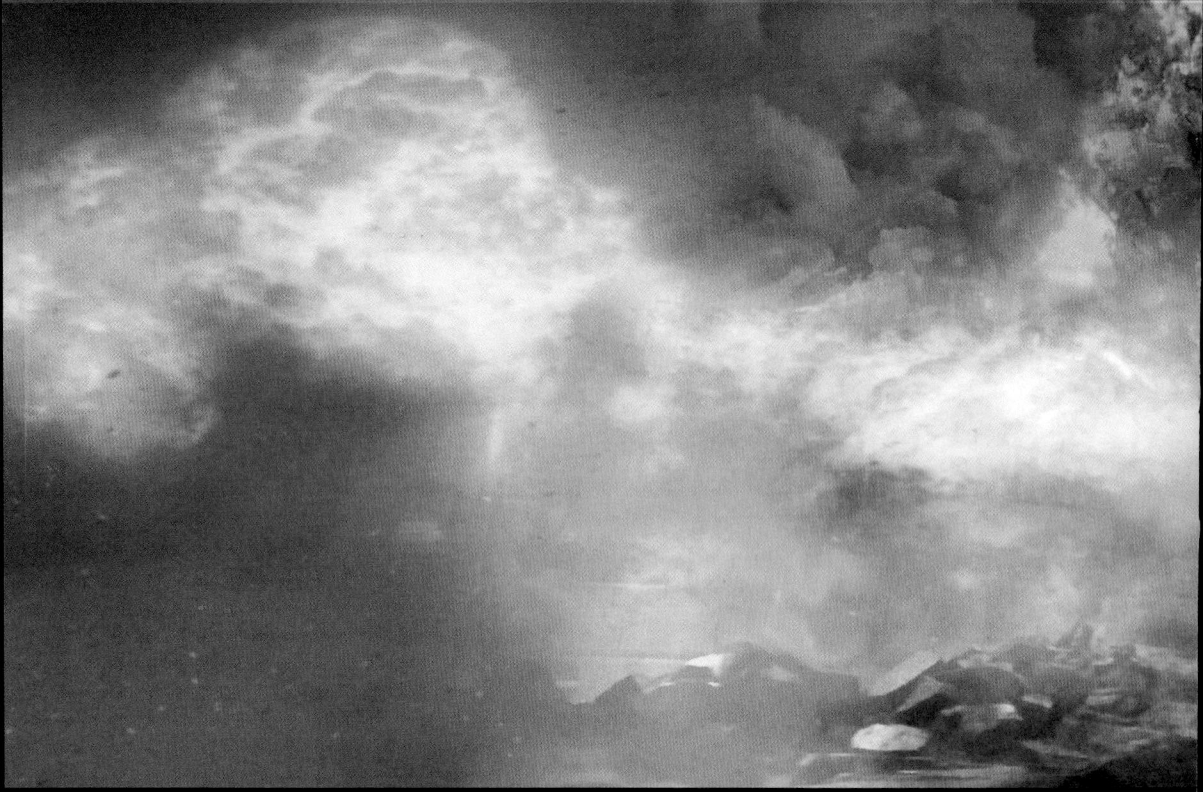

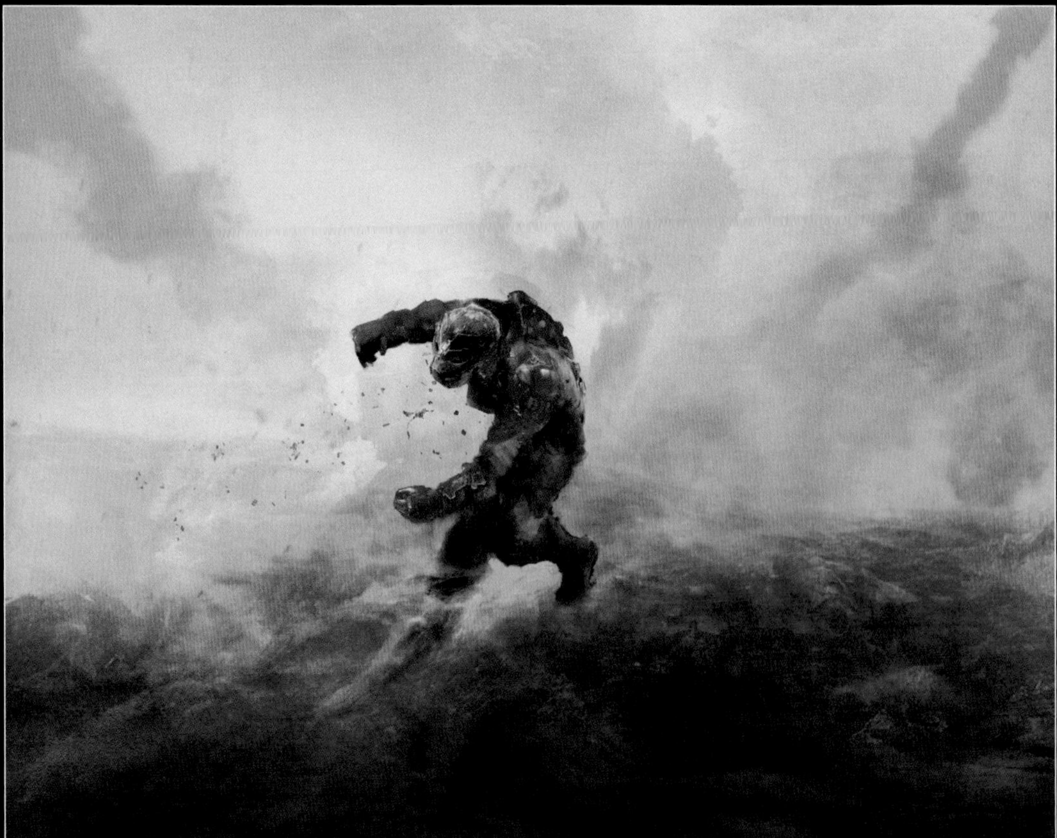

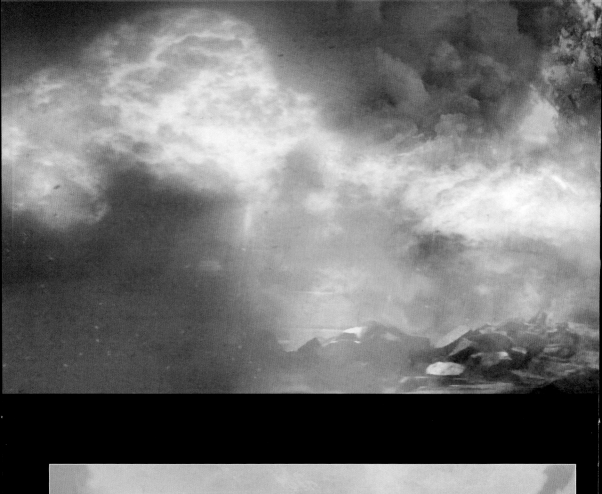

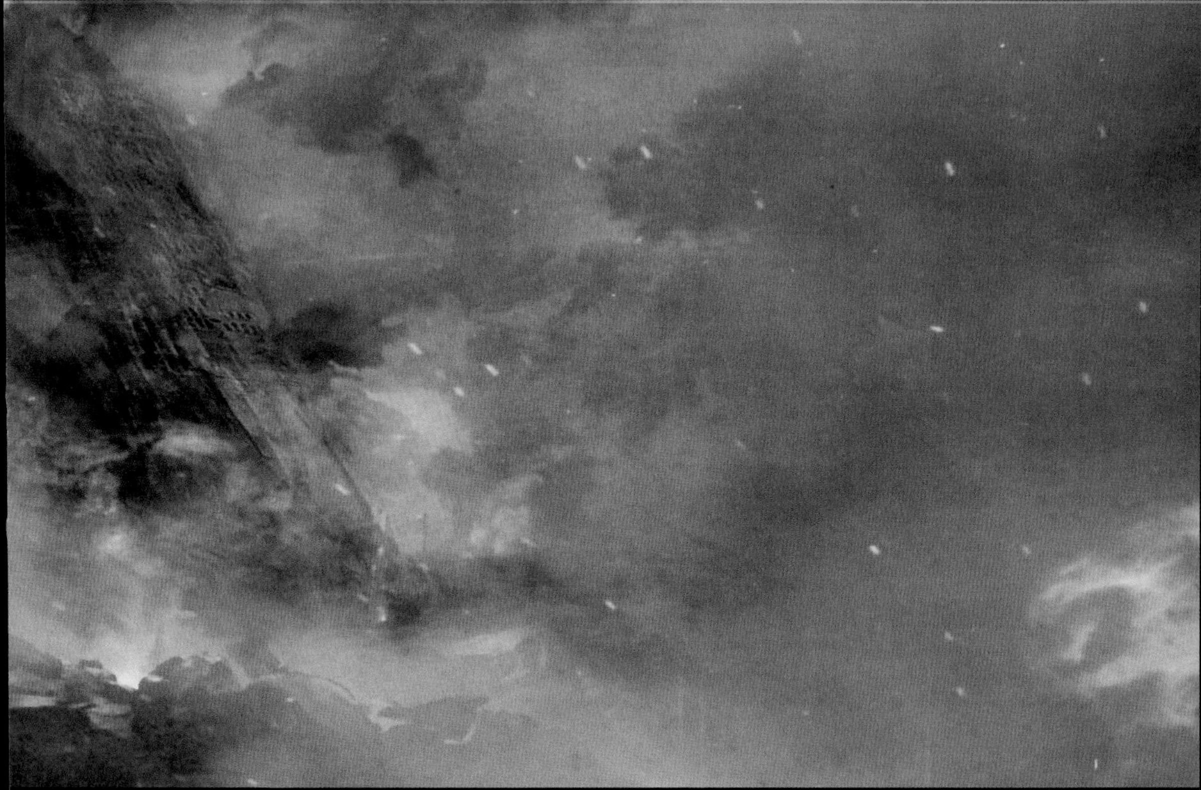

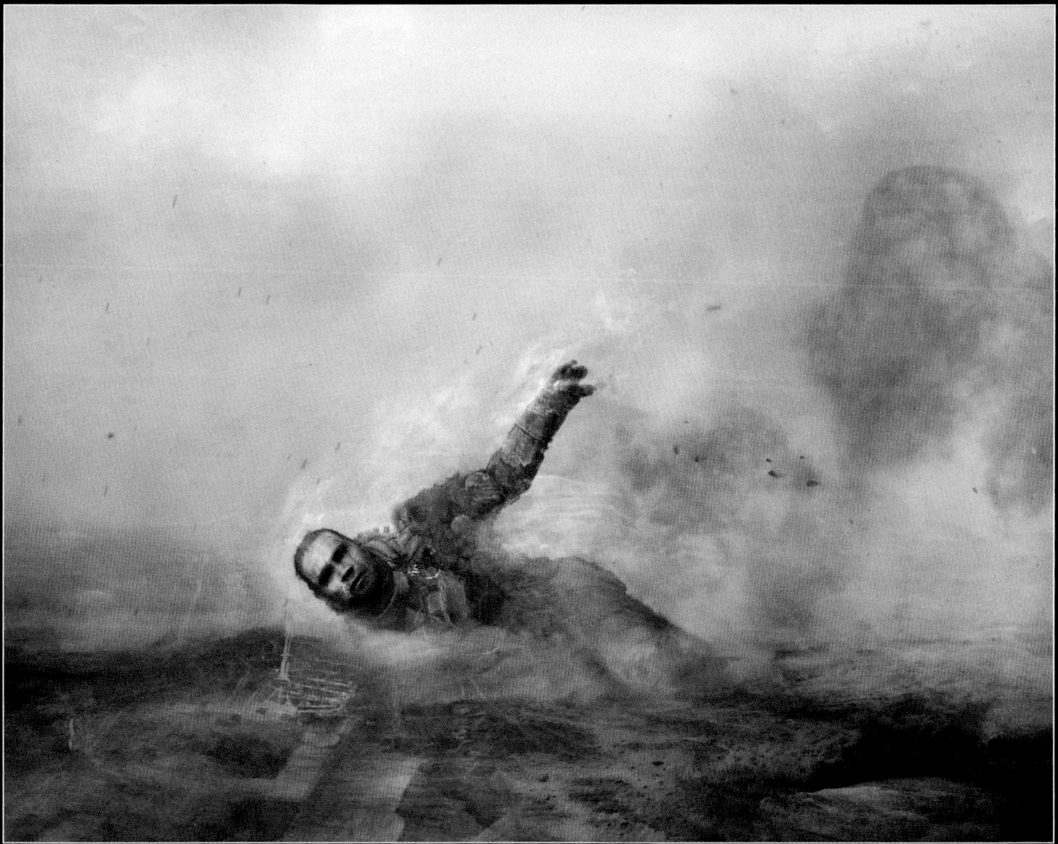

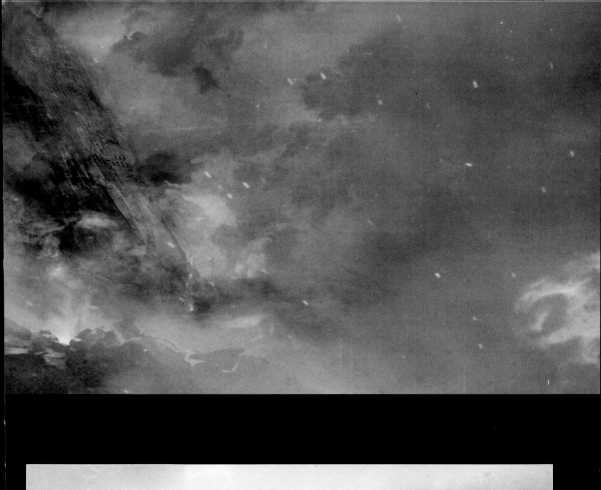

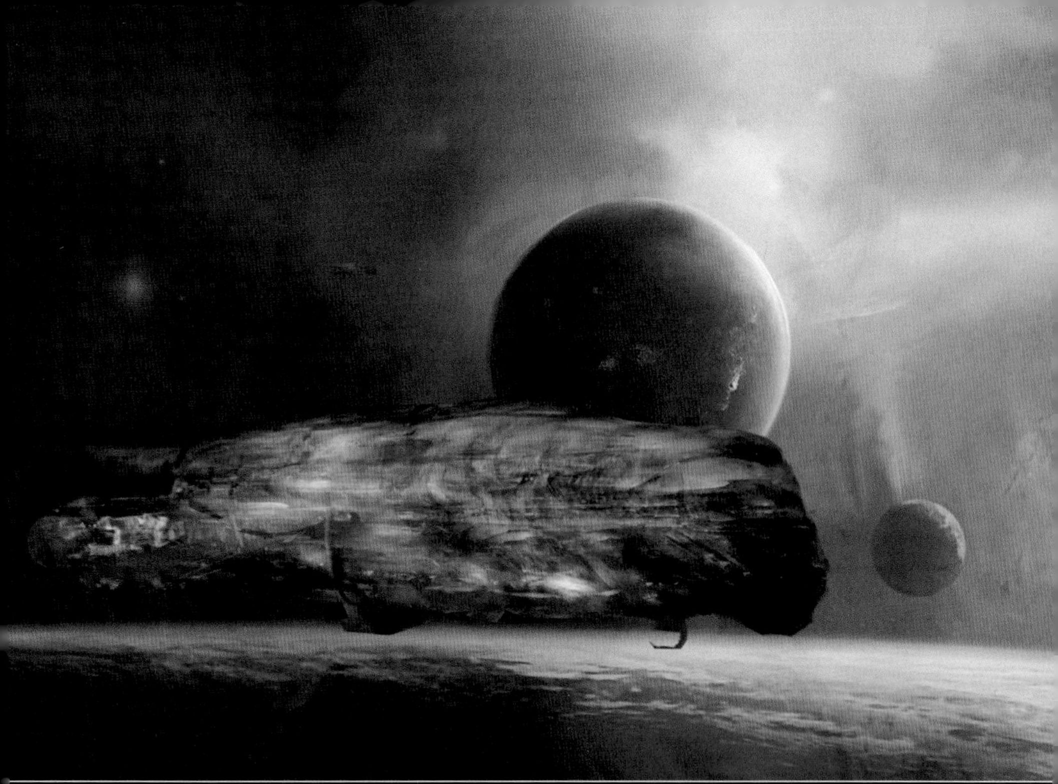
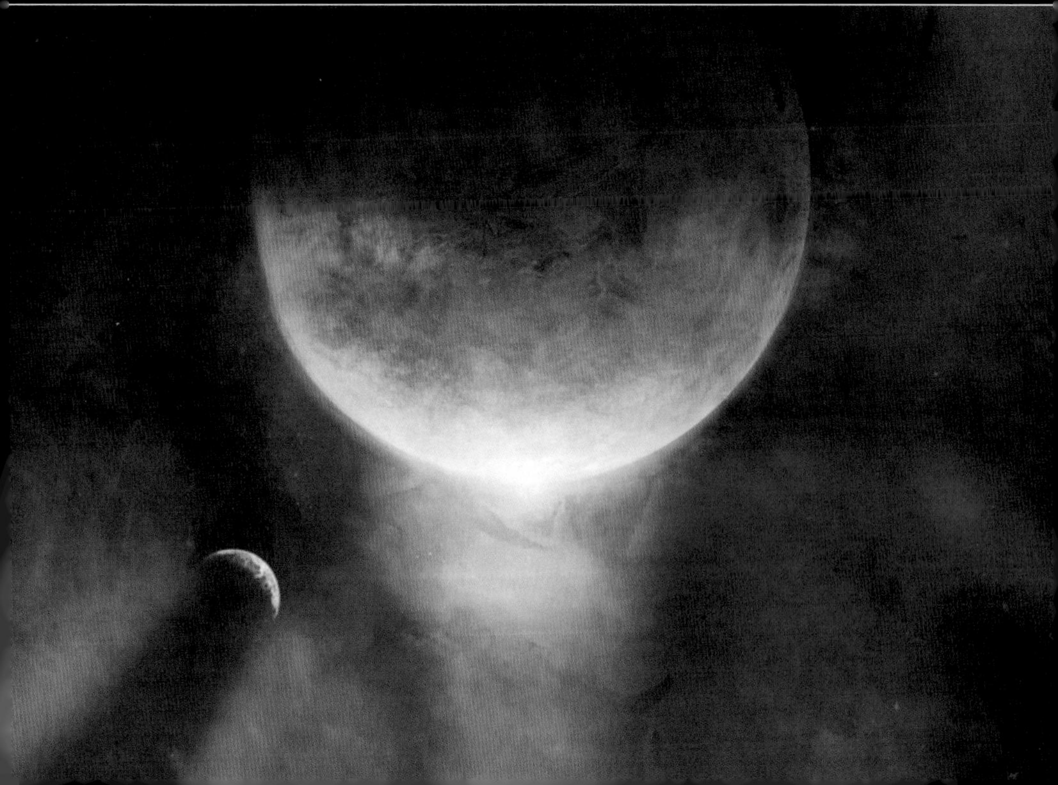

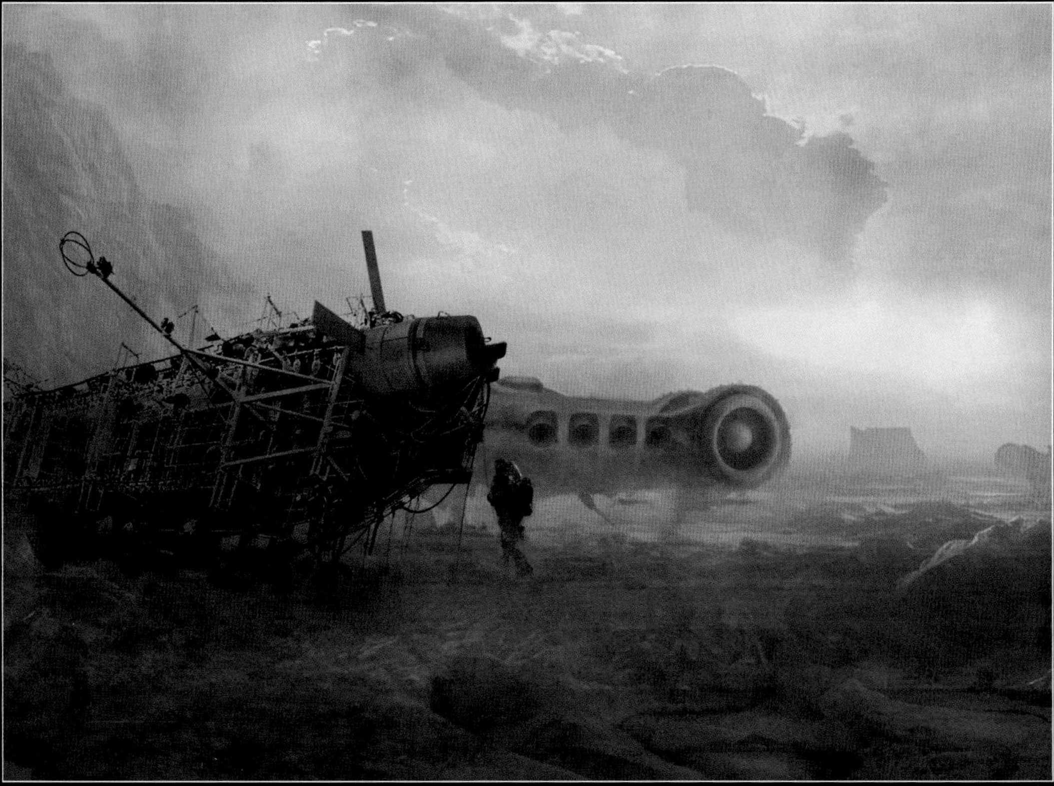

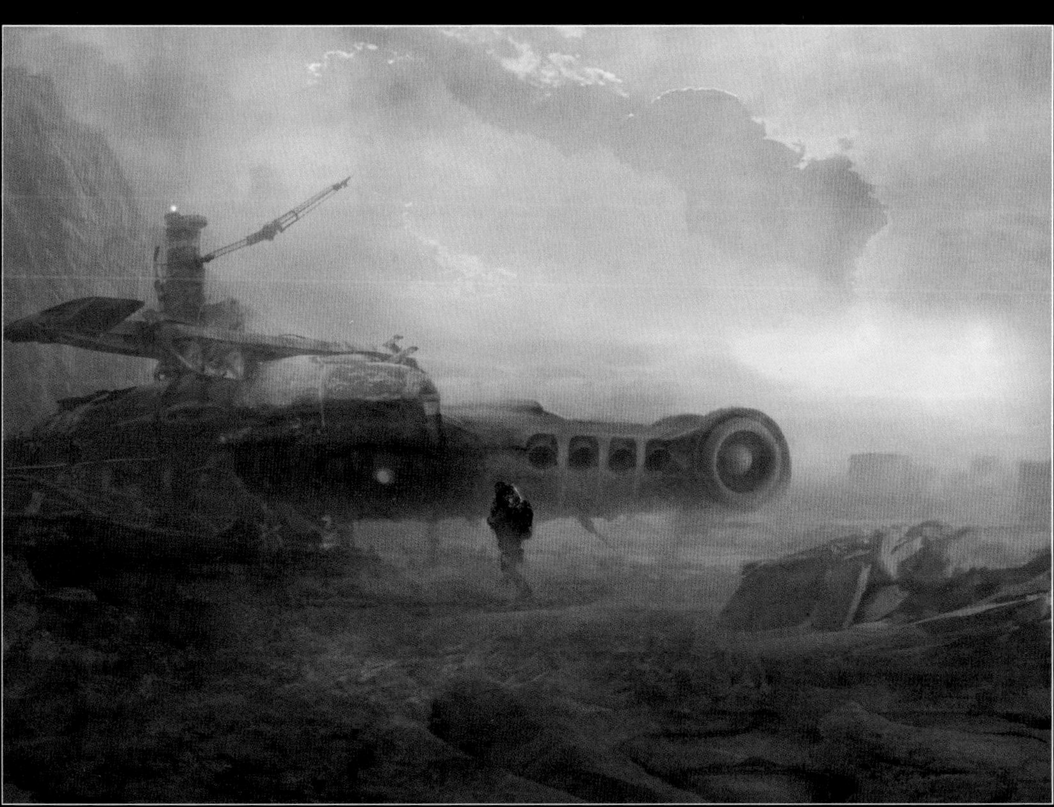

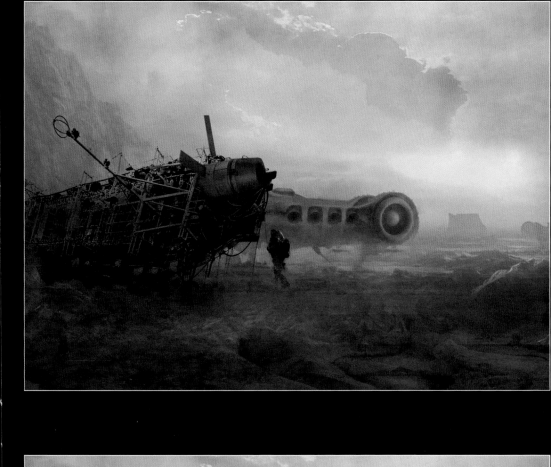

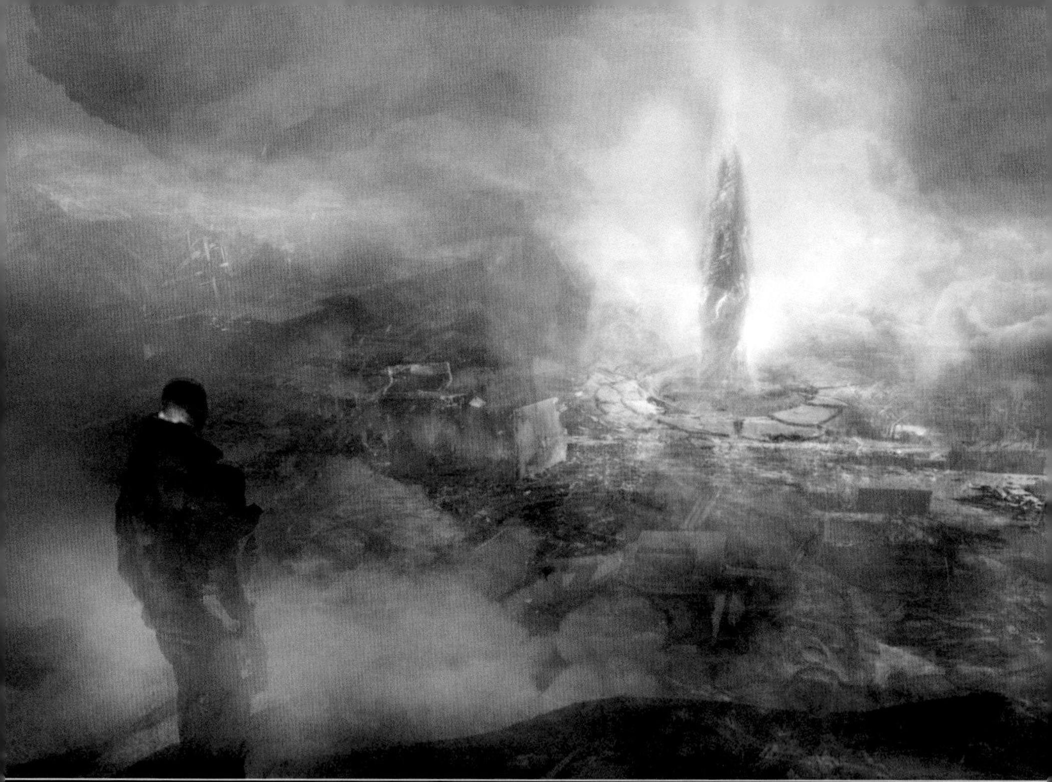

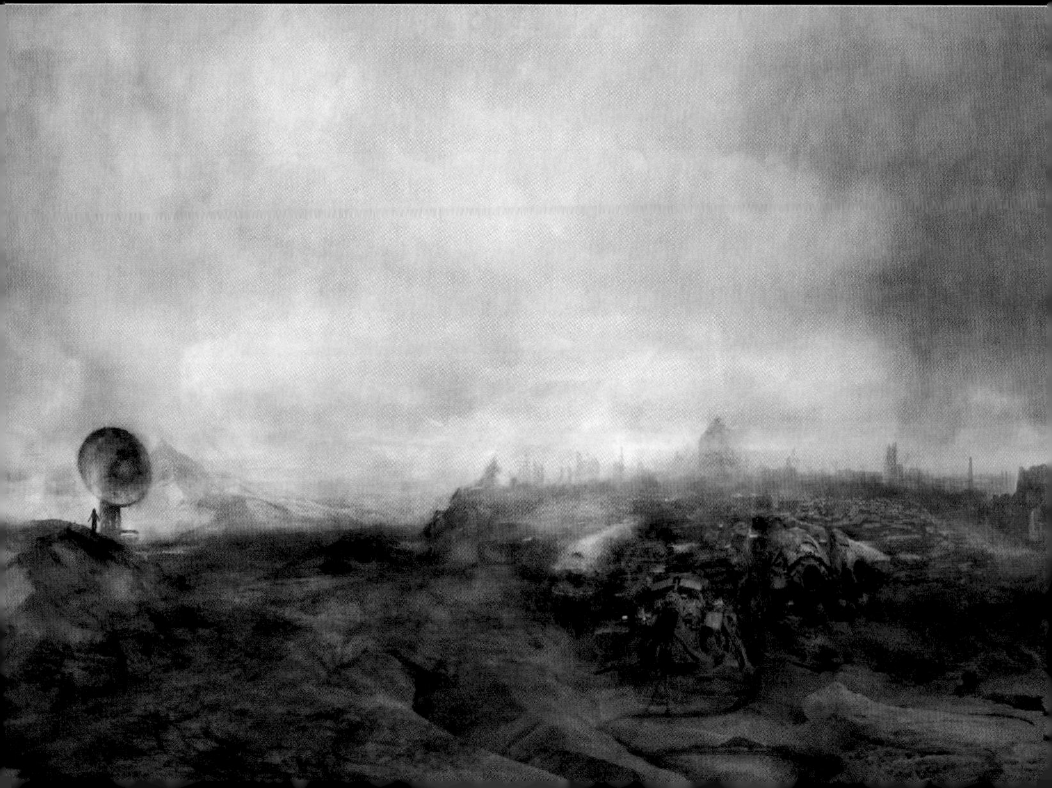

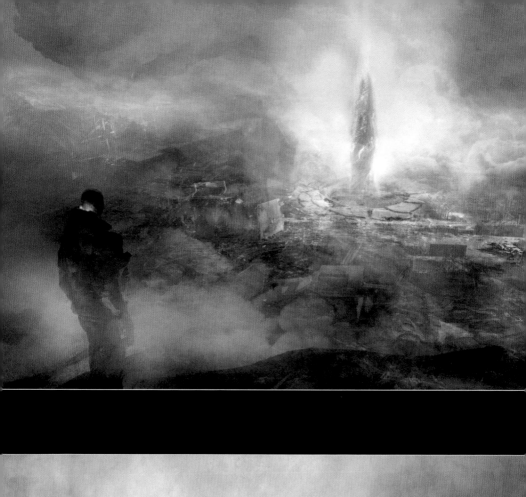

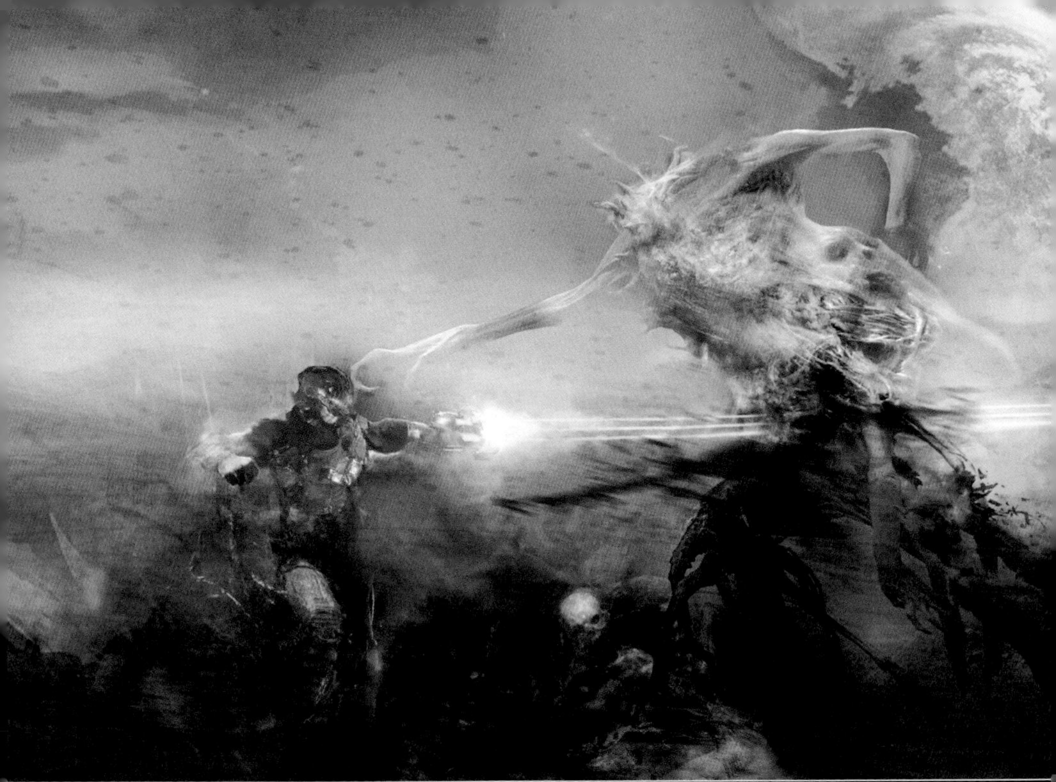

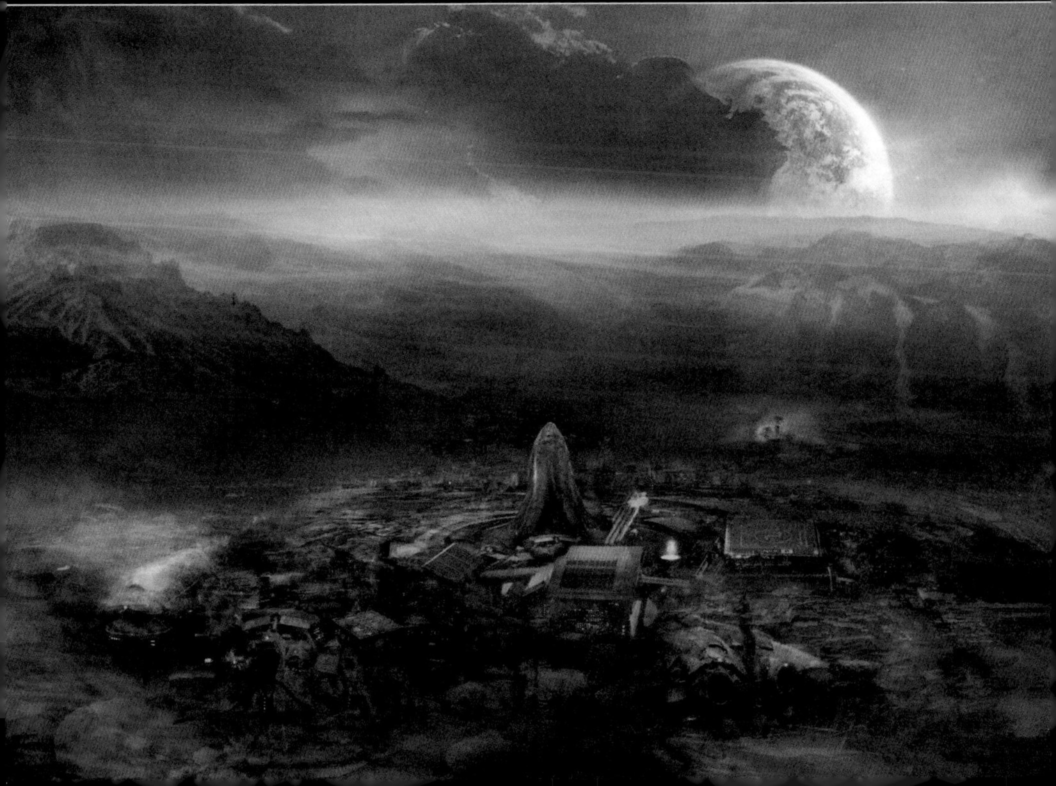

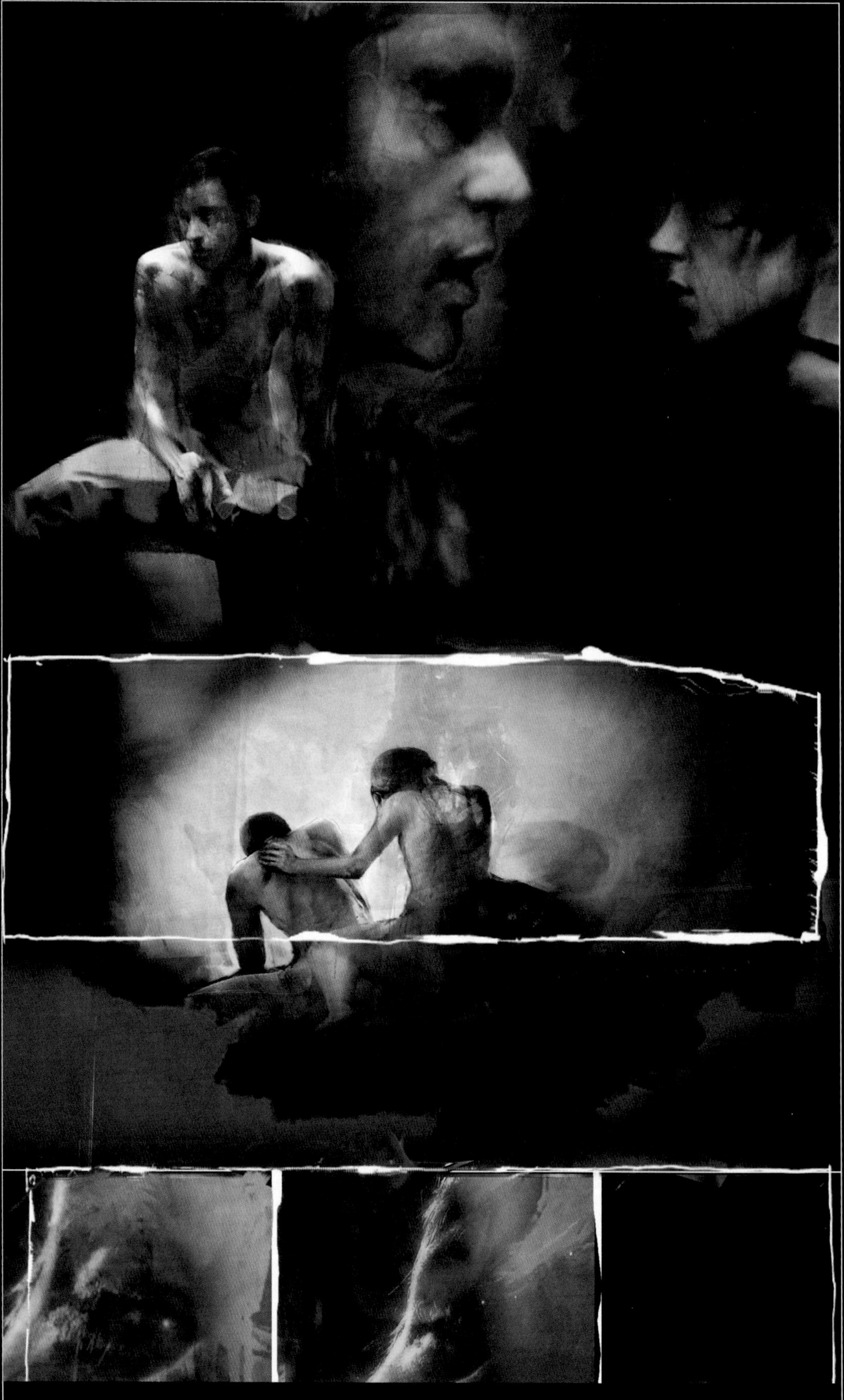

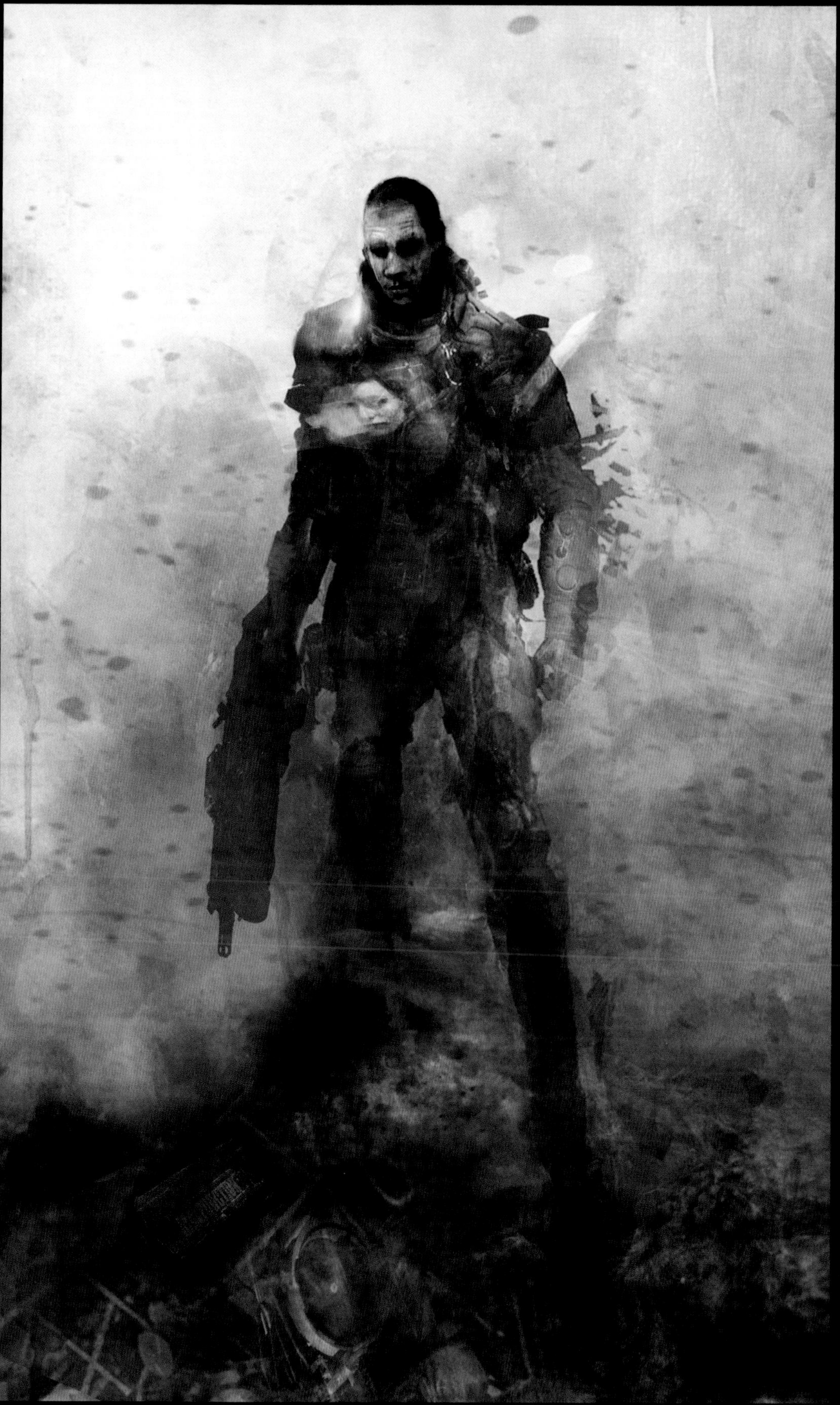

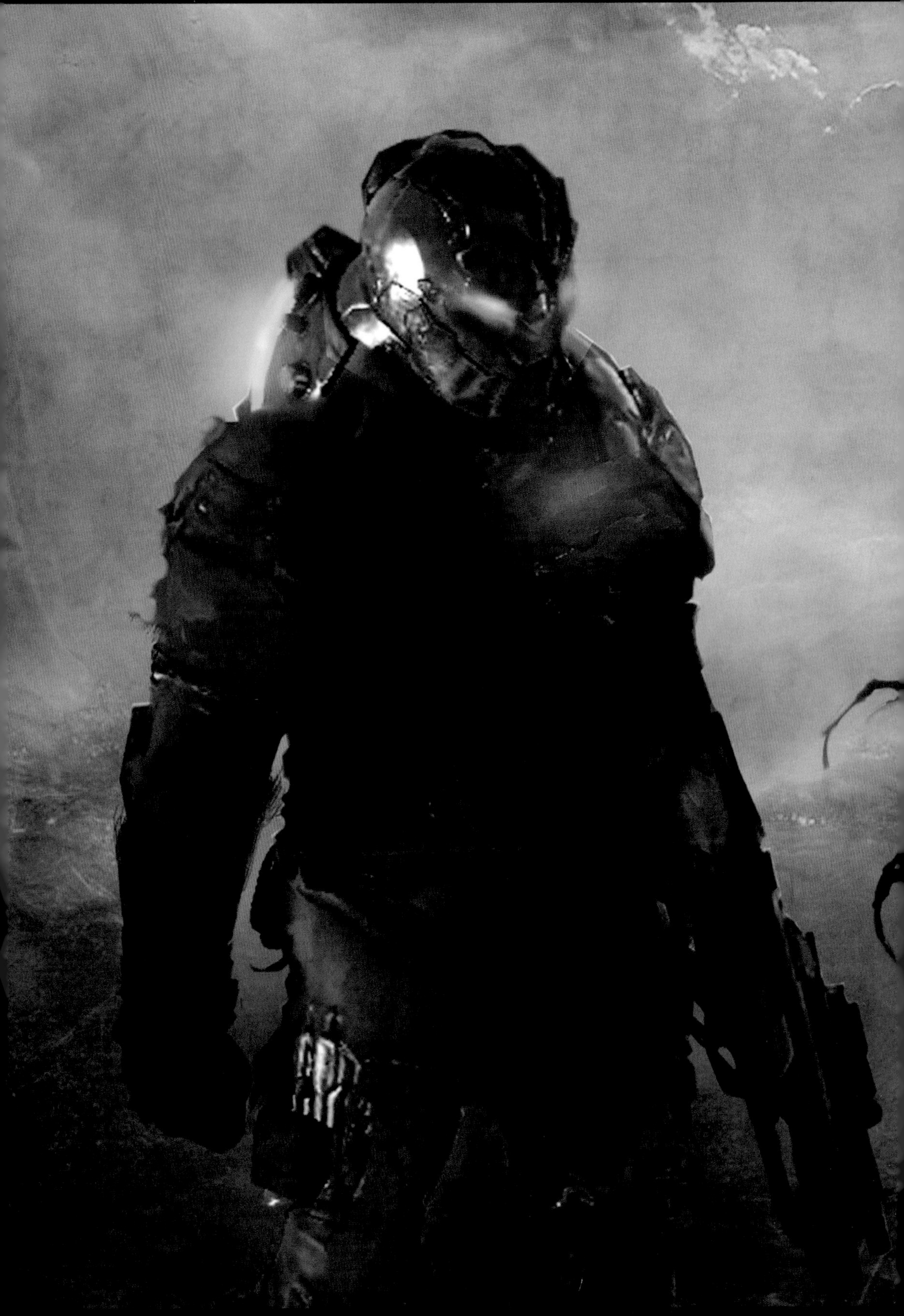

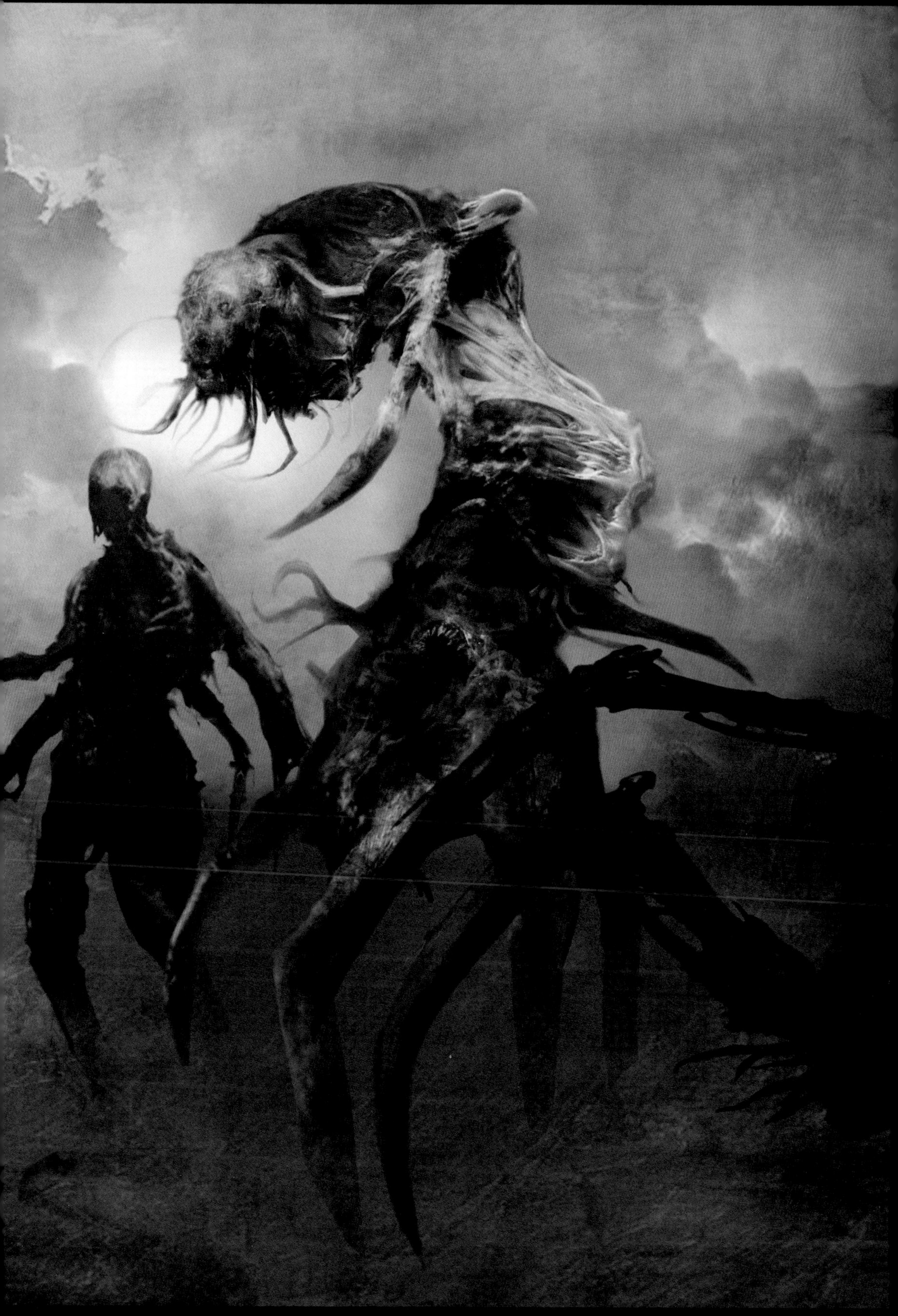

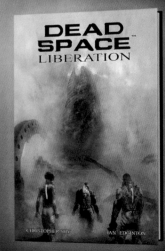